THREE YEARS AT
WAR

THE DIARY OF A CAMERAMAN IN AFGHANISTAN

JOSH FORTUNE

© Day One Publications 2012
First printed 2012

ISBN 978–1–84625–372–0

British Library Cataloguing in Publication Data available

Unless otherwise indicated, Scripture quotations in this publication are from the **New International Version** (NIV), copyright ©1973, 1978, 1984, International Bible Society. Used by permission of Hodder and Stoughton, a member of the Hodder Headline Group. All rights reserved.

Published by Day One Publications
Ryelands Road, Leominster, HR6 8NZ
☎ 01568 613 740 FAX 01568 611 473
email—sales@dayone.co.uk
web site—www.dayone.co.uk
North American—e-mail—sales@dayonebookstore.com
North American—web site—www.dayonebookstore.com

Cover design by Wayne McMaster
Cover Photograph courtesy of Niklas Meltio
Printed by Orchard Press Cheltenham Ltd

CONTENTS

Author's Introduction

Fitting three years' worth of experiences into one book is a difficult task, and as a result there are some things that are omitted and other things that are perhaps covered more briefly than they deserve. For those that are acquainted with my story, I apologize for any omissions: I am attempting to include the key moments of my three years at war—and by including them to a level of detail that I desire, it is necessary that other parts be removed.

This book has been written in diary format, using the notes, pictures, and emails that I collated during my time in Afghanistan. I have attempted to be as accurate as possible with all entries but, as any combat veteran will tell you, perception during a firefight becomes completely subjective. It is not uncommon for five different soldiers in the same firefight to have five different versions of the story afterwards. In piecing together this account, I have reviewed my video footage and everything else that can help me to be as accurate as possible. Some of the names of individuals mentioned have been changed for their own safety.

The key question I asked myself again and again during my time in Afghanistan is this: can God really be trusted? Many of us have asked this question at some stage in our lives—maybe in muttered word, perhaps in unspoken doubt—and particularly so in times of difficulty or danger.

This book is my answer to that question.

Prologue

SATURDAY 6 MARCH 2009

We walk slowly into the village in a staggered column, making our way down the main path. We know the Taliban are here. Everything is deadly quiet. CRACK! CRACK! CRACK! The air is alive with bullets. They are aimed at us. CRACK! CRACK! I have heard about the infamous 'cracks' from combat veterans, but had never imagined how terrifying they would be; like a whip cracking inches from my ear. Press record button on the camera. CRACK! These bullets are close. The Estonians at the front of the column are quick to react, jumping on their bellies and returning fire. I crouch behind Kajaar, the platoon commander, as he assesses the situation. An unmanageable number of thoughts are running through my head. CRACK! CRACK! 'Let's go! Stick with me!' Kajaar shouts, and begins to make his way up front. I am split; very happy to be making my way towards some cover, but not happy at all about the idea of running towards people who are trying to kill me. It takes every ounce of will I have to force my legs to follow him. I am not a brave person by nature—even as a grown man I fear the ball hitting me when I play football. CRACK! That was close. Really close. JesusJesusJesus. I am praying as I run, the word 'Jesus' being the only word I am able to articulate. CRACK! CRACK! Take cover behind the corner of a house with Kajaar and a few other Estonians. This is what it feels like. My heart is thundering; I feel hugely, vividly alive. I want to cry—not out of fear, but sheer exhilaration.

Meanwhile, outside my head, Kajaar is sending some soldiers through the house in a bid to flank the Taliban. I am left with a handful of Estonians, who continue to trade fire with their as-yet-invisible adversaries.

Over to our left, three soldiers in an alleyway begin to yell. I don't understand what they are yelling, but the panic on their faces says enough. Kajaar bellows to the machine gunner on the floor, who begins unleashing a juddering volley of fire at the Taliban position. The three wide-eyed soldiers run to us. One is shot in the leg, the other in the chest-plate of his armour. Seems the Taliban had the same flanking idea that Kajaar did. We are outnumbered. Kajaar receives orders to pull back.

Using the walls as cover, we begin to make our way out of the village. Taliban fire intensifies. CRACKCRACKCRACK! I reach the last stub of dusty mud wall. Going to have to move out into the open and run like a madman to reach the bank where the other soldiers are. Bullets kick up dust on the painfully empty path ahead. I do not want to do this. An Estonian engineer next to me, Ergo, grins at our shared predicament. He pats his buttocks, motioning that I should stick with him as he runs. I nod. Mouth dry with fear. Suddenly, Ergo is running. I break cover and follow him. CRACK! CRACK! CRACK! CRACK! I've never run so fast in my life.

1 A New Chance

7 September 2007—14 March 2008

FRIDAY 7 SEPTEMBER

Feel numb. I'm out of the Army. That's it, finished.

Sitting on the train from Cardiff back to London, under a limp grey sky. This isn't how it was supposed to work out, surely? God, I don't mean to sound presumptuous or anything, but what are you doing? I was supposed to be going to Afghanistan with my mates, but now I'm sitting on this train with a knee that feels like someone has battered it with a sledgehammer. I'm going back—but to what?

So much for being a fit, strong paratrooper—all it took was one tendon in my knee to render me useless, and now they all get to go to Afghanistan without me. Jealous. While they are having exciting adventures and risking their lives, what will I be doing? Wandering around London? I have trained for an opportunity to test my courage in a real war zone for years, and just as it gets near, it is snatched from my grasp. Gutted.

In my head, I replay my final conversation with the officer in charge of my company. He looks like Doctor Who, and so of course that is who he appears as in my recollection. The absurdity doesn't help my mood.

'I'm sorry, Private Fortune—we could take you along with us, but with your knee like that, and given that you have missed most of the training with your injury, I can't see what use you would be to us. You would have to stay behind and guard the camp.'

No thank you, sir, I did enough camp guarding in Iraq.

The train windows grow dirty webs of rainwater.

Arrive in London. Limp through King's Cross Station carrying Army bags. Why, God, why?

TUESDAY 18 SEPTEMBER

Been two weeks since Cardiff. Suppose I should start looking for work, been moping about for a dangerously long time. But what am I meant do? Something in the media, I suppose. Did it at college after all, and recorded a short film while serving in Iraq. The BBC liked that at least—will that help me get a job?

Have not read my Bible for several days now. Why should I? God has dumped me on my own as far as I'm concerned, and taken away the only thing I wanted to do in life.

Still raining.

THURSDAY 20 SEPTEMBER

Offered a job creating video content for small screens on London buses. How heroic. Accepted it anyway. It may be nothing to do with any ambition I have, but I can't deny I need the money. Still living with parents.

Jon, who has been my best friend in the army since we were recruits together in the reserves, calls me. They are nearing the end of their build-up training for Afghanistan, and desperately excited. I grit my teeth and try to make it sound like I'm not jealous. Don't think I manage.

WEDNESDAY 26 SEPTEMBER

See a physiotherapist about my knee. It's not nearly as bad as I thought. She gives me insoles to put in my shoes. 'Make sure you wear them at all times,' she says, 'in a few months your knee should feel better again.'

Doesn't matter, the horse has bolted. It's too late to go to Afghan.

SUNDAY 30 SEPTEMBER

Go through the motions in church today, barely listening. I feel very far from God right now, and if I'm honest with myself I don't really care.

WEDNESDAY 4 OCTOBER

Speak to Jon again; he is heading out in a few days. I wish him all the best, and tell him how much I wish I were going with him. I know for sure this will be a life-changing experience for him. We both felt that our time in Iraq in 2005–2006 was a bit of a joke—lots of guard duty, convoys, and boredom. No action at all. Afghan is the real deal; I know that from the news every day. Jon is going to war, and I'm not going with him.

Go out with a friend after work. Drink myself silly, trying to forget about Jon and Afghan. Fail. Collapse in a field while walking home, sobbing at how it has all turned out. My life is empty.

FRIDAY 11 JANUARY

Another week floats past like a carrier bag in a stream, another weekend after that. The bus people aren't paying me like they should: I'm owed £3,000. Christmas and New Year unremarkable. Life unremarkable. Days and weeks just blur into one great big grey lump. Going to church regularly, or at least attending. Not really there at all.

Email from Jon. He is having fun, but can't say in writing what they are getting up to.

I'm putting on weight. Need to do some exercise. Knee improving. Took its time.

MONDAY 21 JANUARY

The bus people decide that they just don't want to pay me the money owed. I manage to quit and get fired at the same time. Not sure how that works, but the key thing is that I'm now unemployed.

MONDAY 4 FEBRUARY

My friend Fred is home after six months away, and wants to meet up in our local woods, where we used to make stupid movies in our teens. He's been wandering round on his own abroad since quitting teacher training last

August, and is back because he ran out of money. We smash open two bottles of rubbish wine on a fence, and drink them in the chilly dark beneath the dead branches and the howl of jet planes. We laugh and share stories about the various scrapes he got into on the other side of the world, but in the end we are sharing commiserations. Like me, he has no job, no plan, and no idea of what to expect next. It's no real comfort.

SATURDAY 1 MARCH

Play in goal for church football team and we win, our first victory of the season, and the first game in which I concede less than four goals.

I get home, and my mobile phone rings. It's my friend James, who I have known since infant school. He works as a cameraman for a satellite channel.

'Josh, you know I did those military exercises with the Ministry of Defence?'

'Yes.' Last year, James had attended some naval exercises in which he and a few other media folks pretended to be real, rabid journalists, so that the military guys could get some experience in dealing with the media.

'Well, the guy who organized that—his name is Rupert—he's just called me, asking if I wanted to go to Afghanistan to work as a video journalist. I said no, but I thought of you, it sounds like your sort of thing?'

I want to kiss James right there and then.

'Yes, yes it is—could I have Rupert's number?' Voice slightly trembling, trying not to sound too excited.

I call Rupert, but he is driving, and my call is cut short. Send him an email telling him about military background and Iraq video.

Pray for the first time in ages—slightly disgusted with myself that I appear to be using God like some sort of divine vending machine, only going to him when I want something.

SUNDAY 2 MARCH

Check emails before church. See Rupert's name in inbox and my internal organs race to the bottom of my throat. He thanks me for my email, and forwards on the original 'call' on behalf of NATO, it reads:

We have a requirement for two young(ish) video journalists to work with NATO in Afghanistan … It's fully embedded, so inclusive of medical + dental + food + lodging. The role will most likely be minimum 6 months, deploying during March … experience of working with soldiers/military is going to weigh significantly in assessment of candidates.
Thomas

I feel elated, confident for the first time in months. Experience of working with the military? Tick! This, I can do. I phone Thomas immediately, forcing my fingers to stay steady as my phone bleeps out the digits one by one, and he asks me to email him my CV. Sent.

Pay extra attention in church today—it almost seems that my subconscious thinks that God will be more accommodating to me if I do this. I know it's ridiculous to bargain, but I do it anyway.

MONDAY 3 MARCH

No word from Thomas. Worried. Pray.

TUESDAY 4 MARCH

Wake up, check emails. Nothing. Already feels like I've washed out on this, despite rational thinking. Sit by my computer all day, refreshing my email inbox. Wonder whether I should call him—no, that would seem too desperate.

4.00 p.m.—Email from Thomas! It reads:

'Hi Josh—we'd now like to meet you. Can u be at the Paddington Hilton this Friday at 0930?'

The 'u' is reassuringly informal. Thomas, I could meet you on the moon tomorrow if it meant a chance of going to Afghan.

THURSDAY 6 MARCH

Get a text from Thomas in the morning, asking if it would be possible to have the interview tonight at 8.00 p.m. instead of tomorrow. I'm currently doing a week's work in Bournemouth for my friend John, helping to teach some budding young Al-Jazeera employees about using a camera. I text Thomas back: 'Yes, that's great. Josh', still reviewing my choice of words three or four times before hitting send. Slight problem though, haven't got enough money to get the train back to London. Beg my sister, Esther. She lends me £70 for a return ticket. I will have to travel to London and back in one night, as I have work to finish here tomorrow.

5.00 p.m.—On the train. Nervous. I talk to God. 'Lord, you know that I have ignored you since I left the Army, and that I have really turned away from you. Regardless of what happens tonight, I am sorry—and I pray that your will be done in my life.'
Feel less scared now—God is in control. Why did I ignore him for so long?

8.00 p.m.—Walk up the steps of the Paddington Hilton hotel. Still relatively fit, but having to force my breathing rate down anyway. Have just realized that I am not a journalist. (How could I have overlooked that?!) Panic. I foresee an awkward silence when this fact comes up in earnest.
Walk into the bar. Two men with suits wave at me. Can hardly walk away now, so I sit down. Thomas introduces himself and the gentleman next to him—a Danish guy named Teddy.
We talk about my time in the Paras, and Iraq. This is going well. Journalist issue is put down before it even comes up—they have seen my Iraq video on the BBC website, and are happy that I am able to tell stories.
Interview ends. Thomas pulls me aside and asks me about salary— would he ask that if I had just bombed in the interview? Good sign. Say

goodbye to them both. Thomas promises to call me within the next week to let me know if I have the job.

I walk out of the hotel, buzzing. Call my father and tell him that it's looking good, he is excited for me. Can't stop smiling on the tube, people move away from me. Thank you, Lord—still trusting in you.

MONDAY 10 MARCH

No word from Thomas. It's ok—he said 'within the next week'.

TUESDAY 11 MARCH

No call.

WEDNESDAY 12 MARCH

Was it 'within the next week', or 'within the next week or so'? Begin to doubt myself.

THURSDAY 13 MARCH

Oh dear.

FRIDAY 14 MARCH

A call! I'm walking to the local town centre, risking a head full of dust and helicopters already. My pocket begins to vibrate, stomach lurching up again as it has every time my phone has rung this week. Pull phone out, the words 'Incoming Call: Thomas' emblazoned on my screen. Head feels crammed with blood. This is it. Lord, give me the strength to accept whatever he is about to say (but please let it be a yes. Please).

'Hello?'

'Hi Josh. I'm very pleased to tell you that we are offering you the job.'

YES.

'T-thank you!'

'You'll be deploying to Afghanistan with the team in just over two weeks.'

Wow, that's soon. I don't remember the rest of the call. I feel like I am bursting. ThankyouLordthankyouthankyouthankyou. I float the rest of the way to town, and spend the last few coins in my bank account on various supplies I think I'll need out there. I'm pressingly aware that it must seem mad for me to be elated by the prospect of being sent into the world's most notorious conflict—but it appears that this is who I am. I want to be in danger, I want to put my life on the line, I want the adventure. Yes, on reflection, there's probably something wrong with me.

My sadness and shame at not being with Jon and my old comrades feels lifted for the first time in months. I am going to Afghanistan.

2 Arrival

25 March 2008—27 April 2008

TUESDAY 25 MARCH

Lying in bed. Excited. Meeting some of the team at Heathrow airport tomorrow at seven o'clock in the morning. Will be flying to Copenhagen for a week of preparation and training before deploying.

Had emotional goodbye with family. Many tears and prayers. Better now than at four in the morning tomorrow.

Suddenly, hugely nervous. Why on earth am I doing this? Because I want to get shot at. In school I read war poetry, I compulsively watch war films, I have stacks of books about Iraq and Afghanistan. Always shoving myself against the same question: Would I have the guts to do what I need to do while someone is shooting at me, or would I cower away in a little ball? I like to think it's the former, but I need to know. I pray it's not the latter. I see it as the ultimate test of nerve. I didn't get the chance in the army—all that training for nothing. The fact that I'll now be holding a camera instead of a gun doesn't bother me—I never wanted to kill anyone, I just wanted the courage test. This suits me fine. I need this.

The night before going away is always an odd time. Twilight zone. The darkness is a last bastion of normality and solace, with the impending dawn growing heavier by the hour. Change is coming, and no faculty of mine can turn the minutes back. Please be with me, Lord, whatever happens.

It's past midnight when I finally fall asleep. Last sleep in my own bed. Maybe last one ever. When will I see my home again?

WEDNESDAY 26 MARCH

4.00 a.m.—Alarm goes off. Bolt upright. No time to think now, this is a good thing. I want to move. Grab bags, and accompany a glum-looking Mum to the car. In the midst of my excitement, I feel bad for her—she has had to put up with too many goodbyes from me already. Mum, being Mum, runs through last-minute things she has found on the Internet about Afghan as we drive.

'Make sure you don't drink any local water.'

'Yes Mum.'

'And watch out for mosquitoes, have you got malaria pills?'

'Yes Mum.'

'Are you going to be with soldiers all the time?'

'Not sure Mum.'

Finally reach the airport. Swallow tight to avoid crying through the farewell. She tells me she loves me. I tell her too, though awkwardly. I have cultivated a silly voice for times like this, I am not good with such situations.

Jog into the airport with bags. This is it. Meet new colleagues, Will and Mel. Will is two years older than me, Mel four years older than him. We are all very different. My own arrogance astounds me as I catch myself making judgments about Mel, simply because she has a brightly coloured bag. Soldiers would never take something that uncool to a war. You aren't a soldier anymore Josh, get a grip.

We check in our luggage, and get a coffee. Talk to each other warily, sizing each other up. Will has a very technical background, good with a camera. Mel is a journalist through and through, very experienced. My initial impression of her evaporates—this lady knows her business.

9.00 a.m.—Plane departs for Denmark. We sit together in a row, and talk about Afghanistan. Mel reads a book about the Taliban.

12.00 noon—Arrive in Copenhagen. We are met by a Danish soldier who can't help but remind me (both in appearance and voice) of Arnold Schwarzenegger. He drives us to the Danish Defence Media Centre, known as the FMC (I won't even attempt to spell it out in Danish). It is here that NATO TV will be launched, championed by the Danes for at least a year as the viability of this project is gauged.

Teddy, who I now realize is the head of the FMC, welcomes us. He explains that NATO wants to improve its credibility and public image by launching its own channel on the web. The Danes, who have a similar channel for the Danish military at the FMC, suggested it and agreed to run with it.

And we are it. Our job will be to go to Afghanistan, and make content to fill this channel. For the moment, we will be living in the Afghan capital of Kabul, staying at the international airbase there.

Teddy shows us the promo video for NATO TV. Mel and David, a colleague who is already in Afghan, feature in it. Their voices sound very 'news reporter', very professional. I feel instantly intimidated, with my mind lurching back to the stairs at Paddington. Can I even do a voice like that? What if I can't? Will looks at me and grins. I think he's thinking the same thing.

3.00 p.m.—Two FMC journalists who have just returned from Afghanistan speak to us. They show us a map of Afghanistan, and talk through their experiences in Helmand province with the Danish troops. Helmand. The shorthand for everything I feel I need to confront. The other thirty-three provinces in Afghan dull in significance. Helmand dominates the news in the UK, and we have lost almost 100 soldiers there already. Helmand is where I want to go, where the testing and pitiless bullets will come at me.

The Danes ply us with phones, laptops, and equipment. Despite my deeper preoccupation with the task to come, my inner cheap materialist likes this very much indeed.

6.00 p.m.—We check into a hotel, paid for by the FMC. Go to a local pub and watch Manchester United play, an odd slice of normality in the face of our adventure. Return to hotel. Open my small camouflage Bible and read Psalm 27. This was my 'war psalm' while I was in Iraq.

Go to bed with verses one and two running through my head:

'The Lord is my light and my salvation; whom shall I fear?
The Lord is the stronghold of my life; of whom shall I be afraid?'

THURSDAY 27 MARCH

Go to the FMC. Shown the cameras we will be using. Very expensive. Very nice. Practice with them. Again, I like this.

The next member of our team, Dan, arrives. Another real deal journalist: he used to work at CNN. Our work cycle will be about three to four months in Afghan, followed by one month in Denmark to cover any European NATO stories. Dan will be the first to take this shift.

'You'll all be veterans by the time I get there, and I'll look a right newbie!' he laughs, only half-joking. Inwardly I sympathise with him—I would not like to be the first to remain behind.

FRIDAY 28 MARCH

First aid lesson from Schwarzenegger. We are taught how to deal with gunshot and shrapnel wounds. It seems the Danes have a slightly different way of doing it than we did in the British Army. 'Pack to da bone', Arnie says, jamming some gauze into the wound of a foam dummy. Despite the gravity of the subject matter, we laugh. 'Pack to da bone' becomes a popular phrase with us, and is used as a response to any medical ailment, even the common cold.

Wonder if I will ever have to 'pack to da bone' for real.

SATURDAY 29 MARCH

Weekend. No FMC visit today. Go for a run with Dan and Will. Practice doing some of the fitness exercises I had to do in the Paras, including carrying one another one hundred meters. Feels like the appropriate thing to do. Danes passing by on the waterfront think we are crazy. Feel sick by the end of it.

I hope I never have to carry someone for real.

MONDAY 31 MARCH

Leaving for Afghan tomorrow, last full day in a civilized country.

Drive to the other side of Denmark in a taxi to pick up body armour and other useful items from the Danish military's logistical hub, Jutland. Denmark is not a very large country. Cab driver gets slightly lost, and we end up driving around for a while. Will nicknames the driver 'Phileas', a nod to the fictional Mr Fogg who went around the world in eighty days.

Finally arrive in Jutland. Get every injection under the sun. Because we are so pressed for time, I'm sure we are given more than the recommended amount. Oh well.

With bruised arms and heads swimming with half-dead microbes, we enter a large warehouse where we are given armour, helmets (I decide to use my own that I had spare from the Paras—got to play my pro card), socks, flesh-coloured underwear and t-shirts (both skintight and utterly indecent), bags, malaria tablets, and enough extra kit to fill two big green duffel bags.

Try to stay aloof and try to maintain an 'I've-done-this-all-before-aren't-I-cool' attitude. Don't think anyone notices. Or cares.

TUESDAY 1 APRIL

April Fool's Day. We are heading to Afghanistan tonight, and we're very excited about it. Has this day been pre-emptively named for us?

We make sure we are all packed, and pick up some last items of clothing. Dan seems preoccupied with making sure all the clothes he takes with him are flame-retardant. Can't tease a man for being cautious, especially when I think of the amount of flame-retardant gear in the British Army.

Say goodbye to Dan at FMC. I assure him that he probably won't miss much.

7.00 p.m.—Back at Copenhagen airport. An FMC journalist named Lars will be accompanying us out there for the initial part of it, to help us find our feet. He seems slightly eccentric, often breaking into a wide smile when looking at us, and uttering the word 'Brits'. Yes we are, Lars. Yes we are.

Danish soldiers begin to arrive in full camo. Seems slightly odd to me. In the UK, we were never allowed to wear our uniforms in public for fear of terrorism. The Danes seem much more laid back. Slowly more and more of them appear, each one orbited by concerned and loving parents, partners or children. Glad I have already said my goodbyes, this is not a comfortable scene to watch as it is. These guys will be heading to Helmand. Are there any here who won't be coming back?

Board the plane. It's a distinctively civilian plane, run by Pegasus Airlines. The sea of camouflage contrasts strongly with the blue seats. Take off.

WEDNESDAY 2 APRIL

1.00 a.m.—Stop in Istanbul to refuel. Amongst the dappled uniforms of Danish soldiers, see a few Lithuanian troops. Right, time to show my journalistic skills. Walk up to a big, bald Lithuanian officer.

'Erm … Hello, sir. My name is Josh and I'm with the NATO Channel. We're going to Afghanistan to tell the stories of what the different nations are doing out there. Could I ask where you are headed to, what you will be doing, and how you feel about it?'

That wasn't so hard. I can do this journalism thing! Pause. He looks at me oddly, then smiles. His comrade leans in. 'He no speak English.' Ah.

6.00 a.m.—Manage to catch a little bit of sleep on the plane. Wake up— it's light outside. Lean over to the window. Wow. Snow-capped mountains spread out in icy ranks, from here to the haze at the edges of the earth. A great, dry gulf of air and colours fading from stratospheric azure to the opalescent pastels of the icecaps. Breathtaking. God made those mountains. Crushingly, beautifully aware of how small I really am in his great picture. Nevertheless, try to discretely take a photo of myself looking wistfully out of the window, trying to convey with my eyes alone an 'I'm-going-to-Afghanistan' look. That'll look good on Facebook.

9.00 a.m.—Kabul below us. Blocks of houses sprawling for miles, climbing up the feet of the mountains that encircle the city. Everything the colour of dust. Start our steep descent—the nearby mountains allow for nothing less. Wheels hit runway. We are touching Afghanistan.

Kabul International Airport—known as 'KAIA' (someone obviously thought that 'KIA' would have sounded a bit too similar to the military term for 'killed in action')—isn't the most advanced airport in the world. No big tubes connecting us to the terminal. Can't see a terminal, in fact. Climb down some metal stairs to reach the grubby concrete, each step taking me further away from the civilian plane. Further from normality.

Nearby, fifty armed and tough-looking US soldiers stand beside the brooding mass of a US Air Force Hercules plane. I look at them longingly. No Josh, that was your old life. You are not one of them anymore.

We are met by David, the remaining member of our team. Pleasant guy. Earlier assumptions confirmed—this guy, like Mel, exudes journalistic competency. Will I be found out? With David is Kristian, a major in the Danish Army. He will be our liaison officer while we are out here, bridging the perennial gap between civilians and the military.

Collect our bags. Kristian walks us to the Danish National Support Element (NSE) building.

'Welcome to your new home.'

The new home consists of what seems to be large metal shipping containers welded together, with living quarters crammed inside. Sort paperwork, get ID cards, draw out bed sheets. Surprising amount of admin for a warzone. What else did I expect? It's the military!

Will and I draw the short straw. There seems to be a gap in the middle of the block of massed containers, and with admirable pragmatism, someone has cheerily hammered together a room out of wonky planks in said gap. Wonder what happens when it rains?

3.00 p.m.—Accompany Kristian to Headquarters ISAF (ISAF = International Security Assistance Force, the military aspect of NATO's work out here) to sort out some more paperwork. HQ ISAF is about two miles away from KAIA. Kristian puts grenades, ammunition, and a pistol into the pouches of his body armour. Are we expecting something? Put my body armour on. Oh no. It's Danish army issue, but we are not allowed to wear camouflage, as journalists must not look like soldiers. So someone (perhaps the architect of our living quarters?) has seen fit to sew what looks like a dusty brown pillowcase over it. Looks awful. Sticking the Velcro pads around my waist sounds the death knell of any remaining coolness I'd hoped to preserve. Fervently hope none of my old colleagues see me.

Drive out of the gate at KAIA. Out of the protective bubble of ISAF, into Kabul. First face-to-face with the real Afghanistan. Dusty streets. Dusty buildings. Dusty people. Battered Toyota Corollas fill the roads. A group

Kabul in the spring rain. All the dust turns to mud.

of children wave at us as we go past, motioning to their mouths, nodding. Kids did the same in Iraq: begging for food, water, candy … anything. Kristian drives fast, cutting in and out of the Corollas. Out here, niceties of the road are forgotten. Survival of the fittest seems to be the only law—the bigger the vehicle, the more you can get away with. We sit pretty in a four-tonne armoured Land Cruiser. Toyota, of course.

Arrive at HQ ISAF. Fill out paperwork. Lots of different nations represented here: Americans, Canadians, Australians, Macedonians, Italians, French, and Spanish to name a few. See some Brits. Rapidly remove body armour.

9.00 p.m.—Back at KAIA. David and some Danish journalists take us to one of the bars on base. Surprised at the presence of bars—British deployments both here and in Iraq are teetotal. Walk in. Can't help but think of the alien pub in Star Wars. Vast majority of occupants are men, most of whom stare at Mel hungrily. Unpleasant. Is this what this place does to men?

11.00 p.m.—In bed. First day in Afghan done. Feel excited, but it's a world away from everything I knew. Now that I am here and settling, feel less pressure to pray or read my Bible—I got what I wanted, right?

THURSDAY 3 APRIL

Lots of meetings today, even more to take in. Sit in the relaxation room of the Danish NSE, planning out the first stories we will cover for NATO. We can't fly anywhere for a few days until some more paperwork comes through, so stuck doing stories on ISAF bases in Kabul. David recently met a handful of Croatian soldiers and has set up a story to film with them. We decide I will tag along to get the hang of filming a story.

Against all odds, a former colleague of mine walks in. A former Para colleague. Panic. Why is he here?! Shouldn't he be in Helmand?! What is he doing here at the Danish NSE? I am about to get found out for sure. What will he say when he sees me here as a journalist? Soldiers hate journalists! He begins to throw darts at the dartboard.

Furious internal debate. Decide to say hello. He looks at me with surprise.

'Alright, mate. What're you doing here?'

'Oh, erm … Here working for NATO … As a journalist.'

He's mildly uninterested. 'Ah OK, well good luck.'

'Cheers, you too.' Could have been worse.

FRIDAY 4 APRIL

Travel with David to nearby ISAF base, Camp Warehouse. Primarily French and German soldiers here, with a smattering of Croats. Croatian soldiers seem genuinely happy that we are making a story about them. Their country has just been accepted into NATO, and thus the powers that be would like us to mark this event with our new channel. Film them walking around the base, then interview the dog handler. I think his dog is named 'Kent', but this gentleman, gallantly wading through the interview in broken English, refers to it as 'The Kent'. David and I fight to maintain straight faces. Wrap up filming. Given small Croatian flags and lanyards—we are honorary Croats for the day. All in all, a decent start. Despite the genuine human interest underpinning this type of story, it is a testament to how our expectations changed that we would later come to refer to such assignments—stuck on base, not much happening—as 'turds'.

Return to base. Will and Mel back from filming a story about a radar dish. Will's camerawork is very good. Mel's voiceover is intimidatingly pro.

10.00 p.m.—In room with Will. Think he is asleep. Put bedclothes over my head, and practice doing 'The Journalist' voice. Sound slightly like a constipated robot at the bottom of a well. Worse yet, turns out Will is awake.

SATURDAY 5 APRIL

I am beginning to worry that Lars, our Danish media counterpart, might have Tourette's syndrome. In addition to his random and liberal use of the word 'Brits', he is now merrily dispensing swear words in English every time when one of us walks past, cracking into a big grin as he does so.

2.00 p.m.—Go to ISAF H.Q., have to record a piece to camera. Have been dreading this for days. Doesn't go too well—worried about people passing by as I bleat earnestly into the camera. David, who very kindly agreed to film it, assures me that it's not bad. Think he's just being generous, or tired of listening to me chew up the same line twenty-five times.

SUNDAY 6 APRIL

Kristian takes Will and I out into Kabul today. We drive around, stopping at intervals to disembark and film the life of the city. Markets, streets, main roads. Everywhere we stop, kids swarm us. I wonder if any have even seen a

Out filming in Kabul. Note the pillowcase armour.

The Team. From left: Will, Mel, David and Josh.

camera before. We flip the small LCD screens around so that they can see themselves. They are amazed.

Kristian continues to lurk nearby with his M4 rifle and Will and I wear our pillowcase armour, but it turns out we don't need either. This part of Afghan is very different to the Helmand we see on the nightly news back in the UK.

MONDAY 7 APRIL

Paperwork for flights finally comes through. We now have ID that enables us to move around the country. My thoughts immediately go to Helmand. Must find some way of getting there. Two Para battalions are working in the south, in Helmand and Kandahar. Wonder if I can link up with them somehow? Would be sure to get myself caught up in combat that way, surely?

WEDNESDAY 9 APRIL

Sitting on a Hercules with Kristian, flying down to Kandahar. Feels weird being on one of these—last time was during my parachute jump course. Smell of hydraulic and coolant fluid invoking strong memories of fear. Odd how smells do that.

6.00 p.m.—Arrive at Kandahar Airfield (KAF). Biggest base I have ever seen. Apparently the perimeter is 16km—virtually a small town. Kristian and I grab some food and bed down in the Danish area of camp. I catch my first glimpse of the infamous KAF 'boardwalk'—an area in the centre of camp that resembles a low budget holiday destination; it is adorned with a volleyball court, hockey ring, and various unhygienic-looking franchise fast food and coffee containers. A few dozen kilometres away, some troops are fighting for their lives in abject conditions, while others here drink coffee and eat Pizza Hut. Welcome to Afghanistan, experiences may differ.

THURSDAY 10 APRIL

I find out that one of the Para battalions is based here, conducting their missions out of the airfield. They hold an unmistakable air of disdain for the boardwalk patrons. Must find a way to get with them, I think, as I drink my coffee and order a meat feast pizza.

SATURDAY 12 APRIL

Finally get my chance. Walk over to the Para camp. Burly, tanned men, complete with the almost obligatory adornment of handlebar moustaches, sit around outside their command room. Feel intimidated. Their press officer, Ian, is actually a really reasonable chap who arranges a trip for me to go out and see the work that 'the boys' are doing in a place called Maiwand … which is right next to the Kandahar-Helmand border. Excited.

SUNDAY 13 APRIL

Have an early helicopter flight this morning. I go to the HLS (Helicopter Landing Site) and meet the Colonel and RSM (Regimental Sergeant Major) of 3 PARA, the battalion that I am going to be filming. They are flying out to the forward location too. We are standing on heat-softened tarmac, sweating in our helmets and body armour, waiting for the RAF Chinook helicopter crew to start the craft's massive twin engines. The RSM, a man who earned a fearsome reputation during the brutal 2006 deployment here, looks at me for a moment, and then mutters to the colonel. Unfortunately I can hear every word. 'Look at his helmet.' Oh. No. My plan to look cool with my Para helmet has backfired stupendously. It was a well-known fact that after 2006, Paras were not allowed to wear their iconic helmets on deployments anymore—there was a concern about their level of ballistic protection. This upset many Paras who, like me, often value looking cool over pragmatism. Having an upstart journalist turn up wearing one—when they themselves aren't even allowed to—comes across as a pretty heinous insult. Josh, you spectacular fool.

Regardless, try to pretend I haven't heard. Thankfully, the Chinook starts up, and we are ushered in by the flight crew. Take off.

After a thirty-minute flight over featureless ochre desert, the RAF crewman holds up two fingers. Two minutes until landing. I make sure my bags are ready to go. Nobody wants to be 'that guy' who keeps a helicopter stuck on the ground in hostile terrain while he blunders around with his bags. Touchdown. Heat. Light. Dust. And within a blink, the Chinook is gone. Pick myself up, and look around.

We are in a giant square, which is formed by the ubiquitous Hesco blocks—big wire mesh cubes filled with dirt, a common sight in modern conflict zones, which offer protection against most forms of enemy fire. A group of soldiers are waiting for us. It's a short walk to their base, an old Afghan police station. Scores of tanned, lean young guys are busily fortifying the walls with sandbags. A few cast a wary eye at me. Wonder if there is anyone that I know here—unlikely, as I was in a different battalion. I am given a camp bed in the porch area in front of the main station building. It is in the shade, but acts as an almost perfect wind tunnel. As a result my hair, skin, clothes and gear soon adopt a rather sandy colour.

Recognize a captain who was part of my company in Iraq. 'Hello, Fortune. You've put on a bit of weight, haven't you?'

MONDAY 14 APRIL

My first patrol today. I am told that it will be about eight kilometres. The sun is already baking cracks into the earth. I stand around with the other Paras about to head out, until the Afghan soldiers arrive. A huge part of the effort here is to get Afghan and ISAF forces to go on patrol together, with the aim of ensuring the Afghans can learn from their more established counterparts. Eventually, we are told, the Afghan army and police will take over the security of their own country, and NATO can leave.

Despite my enthusiasm to believe this, the appearance of the Afghan soldiers is quite shocking. Their uniform—if it can be called that—is all over the place. They are holding their weapons wrong. Some of them are holding hands. A Para makes a joke about the appearance of the Afghans. Everyone laughs. I join in too. He turns to me with a withering look. 'I don't know why you're laughing mate, you look just as bad.' It appears my efforts to look like a cool reporter have fallen short. The moment stays with me.

The patrol that follows is a long one. In terms of walking distance covered, it actually turns out to be the longest patrol I conduct during my entire three years here. It is unfortunate that it comes at a time when I am so unfit from all my post-Para moping.

4.00 p.m.—Arrive back from the patrol. Even my helmet is sweating. Very tired. Remind myself to get into serious training when I return to Kabul. It was a peaceful patrol—lots of scenic views of poppy fields, which, incidentally, were being harvested for their opium. 'It's not fighting season yet,' a young lieutenant informs me, 'they are all harvesting their poppies. Once that is done, the fun begins.' Lucky the 'fun' is yet to come. If

On patrol with the Paras in the vast poppy fields of Southern Afghanistan.

we had been shot at, I think my legs would have given way. Got some good footage though.

In the lull after the exertion, I leaf guiltily through my camouflage Bible out of a sense of spiritual duty. I brought it with me because it just 'felt right', and it had been with me for years. But deep down, the words in it do not really connect with me. I am where I want to be in life, and the words within seem—at best—a comfort blanket thrown on top.

WEDNESDAY 16 APRIL

Flying back to KAF, and then onto Kabul. Another quiet patrol yesterday to the district centre, where I was shown a clinic. Filmed it—NATO loves things like this. Very humanitarian. Public image and all that. Had to record the interviews to go with my story this morning. I am quite a shy person, and approaching a group of mildly hostile men to ask them to talk to the camera was a rather intimidating prospect. I procrastinated until there was one hour left until my flight out of there, then rushed through the job. Can't help but feel a tad disappointed that I haven't see any combat— but come on, this is Afghanistan, it can't be that long until I see some, right?

FRIDAY 25 APRIL

Have been back in Kabul for a few weeks now. Edited the Para story. Was informed by Lars that it was verging on being overly biased in favour of the Paras. I think he has a point.

One of the first questions that a person gets asked on the Kabul social circuit is 'How long have you been here?' When I reply 'just under a month', I receive a weary smile, laced with condescension. Time served here, it seems, is the currency of credibility in these parts.

As for my credibility ... well, going out drinking with the team most nights has earned me the nickname 'Slosh Josh'. How formidable.

10.00 p.m.—Get back to base after a night out in the city. Drunk again. Receive a text from Dad: 'Mum has had a serious stroke. Please pray.' Shocked. Vision becomes blurry with tears. Dear Mum, who dropped me off at the airport a month ago, and told me she loves me—now a victim of a serious stroke? She is always so healthy and active—why is this happening? Within an instant, I find myself praying fervently for the first time since I got this job. Angry at myself for treating God like a vending machine again, but continue to pray. Phone home. Mum answers. What?

'Mum, Dad said that you had had a stroke ...'

'Me? No! His mum. Dordi.'

'Oh.' Relief courses through me, chased by instant guilt and regret. Dordi is a sweet old lady who has been very good to us grandchildren. It strikes me how untouchably far away my home and family really are, and the alcohol is not helping me deal with this rationally. Nevertheless Will, who is now back, speaks to me with sympathy. He is also suffering through confusion and regret, having just ended a three-year relationship. Morale low all round.

My wooden room.

SATURDAY 26 APRIL

Afghan Independence Day tomorrow. There will be a big military parade in Kabul. We are told to go and film it. Surely this parade will be a target for the Taliban? No, we are told, it will be fine. We are, however, too late to get the right accreditation to secure a spot on the media list.

SUNDAY 27 APRIL

Taliban attack the parade and attempt to assassinate the Afghan President, Hamid Karzai. At least four dead, eleven wounded.

3 The Bubble

5 May 2008—31 July 2008

MONDAY 5 MAY

2.30 a.m.—BOOOOOM! Wake up. What was that?! Sirens. Footsteps running. Our base in Kabul has been rocketed. Sirens continue. We are supposed to go to the shelter at times like this. Normally I would, but I have to be awake in two hours. Sounds blasé, but this is one thing I became familiar with in Iraq—universally, rocket attacks almost never result in fatalities. Can hear the Danish NSE Commander, Bo, systematically going through all the rooms, making sure everyone has gone to the shelter. The problem is that the Taliban never fire after the siren, and therefore the shelter becomes an hour-long sweat odyssey with very little protective benefit. And I need sleep. Bo is getting closer and closer to my room. Will be in trouble if he catches me. Ridiculously, decide to hide in cupboard.

My door opens, his shadow spilling into the room, lit from behind like a cheap horror film effect. He takes one step in. 'Hello?' I hold my breath. He pauses. Oh goodness, if he catches me, what on earth am I going to say? That I was in my cupboard looking for clothes? Door closes, no excuse needed. Phew. I tiptoe up to door and lock it. Back to sleep.

4.30 a.m.—Phone begins to vibrate furiously, hauling me awake with its unwelcome honk. Time to go. Groggily drag my clothes on and grab my bags. Walk out of the camp's front entrance. The Belgian guards are looking nervous, pointing their weapons at a dark car that is sitting nearby with its headlights on, looking ominous. Suicide bomber? No lads, it's my taxi. Question my own sanity. In the military, all movement outside the base falls down to two primary maxims: travel in numbers, travel with weapons. I am alone and unarmed, about to get in an Afghan taxi, and travel through dark valleys and mountain passes to get to Bagram, a large, sprawling US base ninety minutes' drive away. Getting a flight there is a difficult prospect, and so we have decided to use KH Services, the Afghan taxi company that have been our chariots to and from nights out in Kabul. This is one step further. Ahmad, one of the drivers, greets me cheerily as I get in the car. He looks tired. So would I, if I had to wake up this early to drive a man into the wilderness, and grumpier to boot. We depart. The dark streets are empty. After a while, we leave the outskirts of the city. The only light now comes from the dust-choked headlights of the battered taxi. Potholes riddle the roads, while mountains loom, black and brooding, in the distance. Suddenly see a group of men wearing dark clothing illuminated in the dust. They are blocking our path. They are carrying weapons. Heart clenches. Are these Taliban conducting an illegal checkpoint? If so, an unarmed, isolated Westerner will be an absolute gift to them. They motion for us to stop. I wonder if Ahmad can hear my heart beating. He cranks down his window. A weathered face looks in. I catch a slip of blue material beneath his brown cloak. Are these Afghan police? Might be out of the woods, although corruption in the police is a big issue here: I might be on the receiving end of a 'shakedown'. I throw caution to the wind and produce my ISAF pass. 'ISAF, ISAF' I say. If this is a policeman, then as an ISAF member, I am technically his ally. If he is a Taliban, then I am his mortal enemy. Ahmad nods and echoes my assurance, with a brief burst of Dari to accompany it. The weathered face pauses, then nods. 'ISAWWF, guud.' We are allowed through. Relief.

6.00 a.m.—Arrive at one of the Bagram entry control points. It's a long walk past the Americans' initial line of defence (private security contractors) to reach the camp. A confused and angry US guard has no notification that I am arriving, so I remove my phone from my pocket to call my contact in Bagram. 'PUT THAT PHONE AWAY!' yells the guard, who knows phones are often used as triggers in suicide bombings. I, however, am a British guy wearing khaki clothing with an ISAF security-cleared badge around my neck. Irritating. Finally get into the base.

TUESDAY 6 MAY

Find myself in Mehtar Lam, the capital of Laghman province—one of the eastern parts of the country that comes under US jurisdiction. Quite excited, as this is my first embed with US forces. In my former Army days, we often wondered about the calibre of our allies—it seems I will get first-hand experience on patrol tomorrow.

WEDNESDAY 7 MAY

Get up early for a patrol. It's not quite as 'cool' as I hoped it would be—it's a case of walking to an Afghan police checkpoint, about eight hundred meters away from our base. Compared to the memory of the eight-kilometre slog with the Paras, this hardly seems intimidating. A US sergeant, T, turns to me. 'Hey reporter, you think you will be OK with this distance?' Internal flare of indignation. It seems that these soldiers, like I used to, think that all media people are inherently weak. Resolve to introduce myself as a 'cameraman' in future embeds. Can't stomach the name 'reporter'.

2.00 p.m.—Get back from the patrol. It was a sweaty affair, but over fairly even ground. It looks like the laps around Kabul airbase with a heavy backpack are beginning to pay off. Walk past T, who has collapsed inside the gate with heat exhaustion. A medic is putting a drip in his arm.

THURSDAY 8 MAY

Vehicle mounted patrol to Mehtar Lam centre. There is a large shura today; a traditional gathering of elders to discuss important issues. Meanwhile, some high ranking Afghan police and US soldiers will be speaking to some local elders. My first trip in one of the iconic US Humvees. Nervous. In the roadside bomb videos I have seen, it's pretty much always Humvees that get it.

11.00 a.m.—Arrive in the town centre. The shura is about to begin. I set the camera up and start recording. I notice a group of men off to the side with long black beards, dark clothing, and a look of cold hatred directed toward the US soldiers and me. I'd bet my pay cheque that they are Taliban. The US soldier next to me agrees. 'Yeah, probably Taliban,' he says, spitting a glob of tobacco-coloured spittle from his mouth, 'but they aren't carrying weapons, and it's not like Taliban wear a uniform. Nothing we can do about it.' I continue to film. They continue to stare.

3.00 p.m.—Finally returning from shura. Much was said, but it didn't seem to avail much. Mostly the elders looked hot and bored. As we slowly leave the town, I silently hope that the suspected Taliban weren't warning their mates that we were on the way back.

WEDNESDAY 14 MAY

Back in Kabul. Will and I are 'arrested' today. We are playing pool in one of the camp's welfare facilities when Belgian Military Police walk in, conducting ID spot-checks. Despite having been in the country for over a month, neither of us has got in the habit of carrying ID on our person. Our pleas to fetch our passes from our rooms fall on deaf ears, and we are escorted to the police building on camp to be questioned. We contain chuckles while we fill out paperwork, and are let off with a warning. David, Mel, and Kristian laugh at us as we are released. Decide to chalk it up to experience. Speak to Dan on the weekly videoconference we have with Copenhagen. He is going stir crazy, and is eager to get out to join us. It's odd, the gulf that you can feel widening between those 'back there' and us 'out here'.

THURSDAY 29 MAY

The weekly Danish flight arrives, bringing Dan and removing David—who will now go back to do the Europe-based NATO stint for a month or so. I take Dan in his first taxi ride—he is wide-eyed, excited, and nervous. Everything we were last month. It's amazing how quickly people can get accustomed to strange places.

TUESDAY 3 JUNE

Another taxi ride to Bagram. I'll be honest; Afghans drive like lunatics. But it's a testament to their skill that I haven't seen an accident yet. We board the smallest plane I have ever been on; essentially a minibus with ropey-looking wings. Our destination is the idyllic Bamiyan province, and the Kiwi soldiers that patrol the picturesque landscape. Bamiyan was the site of the two giant Buddha statues famously dynamited by the Taliban for being idols in 2001, provoking an international outcry. The plane putters above the frost-bound mountains that separate Bagram and the province, and once again I am sent reeling by the view. My ears are popping horrendously—it seems that there is little or no internal pressure in this rattling machine.

10.00 a.m.—Touch down on gravelly runway opposite the rubble where the Buddhas stood. Verdant green landscape, orange sandstone cliffs, white and purple mountains thrusting cold into the sky. This seems a world away from the hot, dusty south. The locals here are friendly. The Kiwi soldiers patrol without helmets. Yet I am reminded I am still in Afghanistan when I am given an introductory brief: I can leave the base alone to run up the hill nearby, but I have to stick to the path roughly outlined with painted white stones. Apparently, the Soviets blanketed the surrounding terrain with mines during their time here in the 1980s, and while the white-stone path has been cleared, there are more than a few lethal relics left in the ground.

WEDNESDAY 4 JUNE

9.00 a.m.—Going on a vehicle-mounted patrol to a school project, about an hour's drive away. Again, struck by the soft-skinned (unarmoured) vehicles, and lack of helmets—Kandahar and Helmand feel like they belong to another country. To date, the most beautiful drive I have ever been on—every turn in the road revealing a startlingly beautiful vista that alone would warrant a tourist pilgrimage to this province. My video camera laps it up.

11.00 a.m.—Reach the school—which is really a couple of heavy-duty tents pitched alongside one another—and begin to film the Kiwi Provincial Reconstruction Team showing off their project. In a country where education is limited, it is indeed impressive. A pretty young Afghan girl—barely out of her teens—points at a blackboard, as thirty children copy the letters down into their books. Several look at my camera with wonder. I perform the screen flip trick so they can see themselves. Laughter. I haven't seen many mirrors during my month in the country; I wonder what the children make of seeing themselves in high definition.

4.00 p.m.—Back at the base, and fancy a run up the hill after sitting in a vehicle for most of the day. Departing the base alone feels very odd, the old 'numbers/weapons' military maxim grating in my subconscious. The gate guards tell me the base closes its doors at 1730, and that I must be back by then. No problem. I hope.

Begin to make my way up the steep paths of the hill, sticking clearly to the white markers. Every so often, I see a suspicious metal object peeking out of the ground beyond the markers. Do not want to put a foot wrong. Listening to my trusty iPod: I am indulging a guilty pleasure and listening to the audiobook of *The Lord of the Rings* as I do about once every year. I am nearing the end, where Frodo and Sam are making the final climb up Mount Doom, to drop the Ring into the fire. Feels appropriate, given my current slog. I started listening to the trilogy back in January, when I was moping, and considering all that has taken place since then, the parallels are comforting. Reach the top of the mountain. Sweating, panting. Oxygen is pretty scarce up here, over two thousand meters above sea level. The sun is beginning to set, bathing the land in a soft orange glow. Absolutely beautiful. Must begin to head back to camp, gates will be closing soon. Put away iPod in pocket, and begin to lope down the mountain—much easier to go down than up!

Finally reach the bottom. Pockets feel quite light. Where is iPod? Oh. It must have fallen out as I ran. The sun has now disappeared behind the distant mountains and the light is fading fast. I cannot leave the iPod. It's not material possessiveness speaking: I had that thing in Iraq, on my parachute jumps course, and my Afghan adventure thus far—I can't just leave it up there, can I?

Cursing my misguided sense of loyalty to a machine, I begin the ascent again with a torch. Josh, you are running up a slope peppered with mines, in fading light, looking for an iPod. You sir, are an idiot. After twenty minutes of searching in the ever-growing gloom, I finally see a square black shape on the floor beside a rock. Pray for the first time in weeks—Thank you, God. The gates are closed when I finally get back, but I am able to persuade them to let me in. Thinking back to what I did, I am astounded at what a really, really stupid thing it was to do. Relieved I rescued iPod though. Lie in bed listening to *Rings* with sense of satisfaction, even though I've somewhat ruined the metaphor by scampering back up Mount Doom for a trinket.

WEDNESDAY 11 JUNE

This has to be it, surely, my first combat embed. Heading east again to the province of Khowst: our contact in Bagram has taken a shine to me, and is setting me up with this trip. There is fighting in Khowst. I have been in the country over two months, and not had one sniff of action yet beyond the occasional ineffective rocket barrage. It's becoming slightly frustrating. This has to be my chance. Taxi. Bagram. Usual problems with gate guards.

THURSDAY 12 JUNE

Arrive in FOB Salerno, the primary base in Khowst. In Bagram, they were selling T-shirts that read: 'FOB Salerno, Rocket City', with a cartoon of incoming rockets into the base. The press officer of the US Task Force—who, incidentally, are paratroopers—tells me that they will get me out to the forward troops as soon as possible. In the meantime, I am put in a room with some soldiers about to go on leave. They talk about their combat experiences. Jealous. Excited.

FRIDAY 13 JUNE

Flight I was supposed to be on today is cancelled due to poor weather. No problem, there has to be one soon.

SATURDAY 14 JUNE

Go to HLS for evening flight to forward area. Black Hawk helicopters land, I run underneath spinning blades and climb aboard. Take off, flying over rocky hills under cover of night. Distant flashes. Was that gunfire? I peer through the window. The pilots and crewmen, their eyes bathed in the green light of their night-vision equipment, begin to talk earnestly. The Black Hawk swings around. We are heading back to Salerno. Thunderstorm. Anticlimax.

SUNDAY 15 JUNE

No flight today.

MONDAY 16 JUNE

No flight. I am beginning to wonder if this is going to happen.

TUESDAY 17 JUNE

Hoping there is a flight tonight.

7.00 p.m.—Walk to HLS in the darkness. Phone vibrates. Text from Mel: 'Slosh you need to come back. Dan has been in a firefight down in Kandahar, and is on his way back. We need to send you down there.' Stunned. Phone Mel immediately. Shocked at what I hear: on Friday, the Taliban suicide-bombed their way into Saraposa Prison, a jail in Kandahar holding hundreds of insurgents and criminals. All escaped. Several hundred made their way into the nearby village of Arghandab, and dug in. ISAF and Afghan forces were sent to take the village back.

Dan and Jamie, an ISAF cameraman, headed out with a patrol of Canadian and Afghan troops and were ambushed by the Taliban, ending up escaping through a river. Jamie was shot in the arm, and two Afghan soldiers died—one shot through the eye. The escape culminated with all fifteen members of the patrol piling into the back of a Toyota pickup truck and speeding away, bullets whizzing over their heads. Dan and Jamie were picked up by helicopter, and flown to Kandahar Airfield.

I pause for a moment; I don't know what to say. Frustration, jealousy, empathy, worry, and compassion boil in my head, all fighting for dominance. If I hadn't been stuck here, that would have been me. Dan has only been here a week or two—he has never even been in a warzone before—and now he has been in one of those situations that you only read about in books, or see in films. What an experience. But how can I dare think like that? People died! Yes, they did, but I can't escape the fact I wish I could have been there. In fact, I'm absolutely gutted. Still, I'm worried for Dan—what must he be going through right now? I ask the staff at Salerno's transport office for a flight back to Kabul. I need to get down to Kandahar. Now. I feel angry with God for the way this has played out.

THURSDAY 19 JUNE

Finally arrive at KAF. Kristian, our liaison officer, is on leave, so a Danish major named Lasse—who is filling in for Kristian—accompanies me. We make tentative enquiries about the ongoing operations against the escaped prisoners. They are wrapping up, and there is no transport available to get to the units conducting the end of the fighting. I suspected as much. I am beginning to see a trend here, I am like a walking bubble—wherever I go, safety ensues …

1.00 p.m.—Call Dan while pacing up and down the KAF boardwalk. He is back in Kabul now. We speak for a while; he talks to me as someone who might understand what he has been through. The truth is that I do not. None of my military experience even comes close to what Dan and Jamie saw, heard, and felt. Dan is editing the story together now, and I am looking forward to seeing the footage. I am also insanely jealous, but now is not the time for that—it's about being there for Dan. He is clearly shaken up by his experience. Who wouldn't be?

5.00 p.m.—Desperate to make something out of this trip down here, Lasse and I reach out to the newly arrived US Marines, who have just begun to conduct operations into Helmand out of KAF. We meet a Marine captain named Kelly—their press officer—who arranges an embed for me with the forward troops next week. Hope and excitement flare. This could be fun.

SATURDAY 20 JUNE

Back in Kabul with the team. Feel like we are really beginning to bond. Everyone is beginning to fall into their natural places without any issues. Mel and David (although he is away in Europe this month) are the natural bosses: mature, responsible, with good journalistic heads on them. Will and I are the 'grunts'—we just want to go and film exciting things—while Dan is probably a mix of both worlds. We eat in an Afghan restaurant named 'Red, Hot, and Sizzling' which, unsurprisingly, specializes in steak. Get very drunk.

TUESDAY 24 JUNE

Back down to KAF again. Third time lucky? I hope. Planning to link up with the Marines tomorrow. I am confident that this embed will be it.

WEDNESDAY 25 JUNE

Slightly disappointed to find out that I am not the only media guy about to deploy with the Marines. There is a crew from a world-famous news channel here who will be sharing my helicopter to Helmand. The cameraman and producer-cum-bodyguard, a former SAS soldier, are really friendly. The journalist is different—constantly interrupting Kelly during her brief to us, talking about his Iraq experiences. When we get to the front, I need to separate from this crew as quickly as possible, or I will be tarred with the dreaded 'reporter' brush by the Marines.

11.00 p.m.—A rocket lands in KAF, delaying our flight. The journalist decides to do a live report to his studio about it, much to the contempt of the Marines who are also waiting to board. As in Kabul, rockets land here most nights, and they rarely hit anything—they are non-events. I stand well away.

1.00 a.m.—We finally take off. It's a forty-five-minute flight to FOB Dwyer, the Marines' base in Helmand. The journalist, sitting beside me, jumps out of his seat in shock when the Marine door gunners test fire their weapons. After a seemingly endless flight in the pitch black, with my posterior growing increasingly numb, we finally land at Dwyer. Despite the fact that we are in the early hours of the morning, it is incredibly hot. I am somewhat apprehensive about the temperatures the daylight will bring. A long slog through the fine sand—almost like moon dust—to our temporary tents. Hoping to get on a convoy to the forward troops tomorrow.

THURSDAY 26 JUNE

7.00 a.m.—Already the sun is high enough to render sleep impossible. Heat. Sweat. Light. I am told that this area is on some sort of plateau that magnifies the effects of the sun. For a FOB, it's quite basic. The Marines seem to pride themselves on spartan conditions, separating themselves from their colleagues in the US Army who are surrounded by creature comforts in their bases.

11 a.m.—Depart on a convoy from Dwyer to a place called Garmsir, which is south of the capital of Helmand, Lashkar Gar. Marines have been involved in heavy fighting there over the last few weeks, clearing the villages of Taliban who have been giving the limited British forces a hard time. I am sitting in an odd truck, which is open topped, but with heavy armour plating on the sides. Not sure how it will fare against an IED. Hope

I don't have to find out. The heat is excruciating. I sip warm water through a rubber tube to keep hydrated.

After a few hours of driving, I finally arrive in the Green Zone, an area of verdant plant life that borders the Helmand river on either side. The majority of the province's population lives close to the river, since life without a ready supply of water in this harsh desert would be unbearable for most. The company of Marines that I am embedding with has set up in the ruins of a bombed-out compound. Wary looks as I assemble my mosquito net and sleeping bag. I hear the word 'reporter' being muttered. Enough of this. I walk over to a group of Marines—fit, tanned, lean, intimidating—and ask them when their next patrol is. Tomorrow morning. Apparently the area is now quiet after a few days of hard fighting. Of course it is quiet—me and the bubble are here. Spend rest of the day sweating in the 'shade' of a broken wall, drinking hot water.

FRIDAY 27 JUNE

6.00 a.m.—Speak to the squad of Marines as we prepare to depart on a foot patrol. I have developed a standard introduction that aims to ingratiate myself with soldiers/marines as soon as possible. It goes something like this:

Them: 'So who do you work for?'

Me: 'I'm a cameraman for NATO.'

Them: 'How long have you been here for?'

Me: 'X months. I used to be a British paratrooper before I got this job, but now I have ended up doing this.'

Them: 'A Brit paratrooper? Cool!'

An ounce of credibility earned, distancing myself from being just a 'reporter'. Job done. It might be slightly cynical of me to shoehorn my past in there, but I think it is important to show them that I can identify with them, and that I am not just some evil hack caricature out to screw them over. We depart on patrol. It's thankfully slightly cooler here than it was at Dwyer, but soon, nonetheless, we are all sweating. At every stop we make, another Marine sidles up to me, and the same conversation plays out. I make sure that during the patrol, I stick to the formation, crouch when they crouch, move how they move. It seems to be working; after the patrol, they invite me to relax in a small, shrapnel-damaged hut with them. We talk, laugh, and banter all day. I ask them about life as Marines—where they live, how they train, what their ambitions are. They ask me about London. Most Americans I have met during my time out here have some sort of ambition to visit the UK capital. For the first time in any of my embeds thus far, I feel accepted.

They tell me about their first few days of fighting. Taliban were everywhere, they say, and they were fighting from house to house. Apparently the Navy SEALs came in and took down fifty insurgents in a night operation. 'You should have been here, man. It was awesome!' Believe me, I wish I had.

SATURDAY 28 JUNE

Another patrol. 'You coming with us, camera dude?' They ask as they gear up. It seems that 'camera dude' is their name for me. Better than reporter!

The heat and tension of patrolling in Helmand shows on a young Marine's face.

We head out. The Marines stop a young man, who one of them believes to be an enemy fighter. He certainly looks very nervous. There are no weapons on him, however, and the Marines are unable to do anything about their suspicions. He tells them that there are 'two hundred Taliban to the north of us, massing for an attack on Lashkar Gar'. The Marines report the news to their command, but privately doubt the veracity of the man's words. 'They always say things like this. Try to feed us false intel to try and throw us off,' a young Marine tells me, 'we just have to take everything they tell us with a pinch of salt.'

SUNDAY 28 JUNE

It really does seem like this area has become benign. Another patrol, which basically amounts to a stroll in the fields. I don't think this trip is going to burst the bubble. Enjoying the company of the Marines though. It's surprising how many of them are married, despite being only nineteen or twenty. A sack of mail arrives for them while we are sitting in the hut. They ask if I could stand and read some of them out, since they seem to think that it sounds better coming from a British accent. Halfway through one letter, I begin to realize that I am reading out a 'Dear John'—a letter that a soldier always dreads—that informs the unfortunate reader that his wife/girlfriend does not want to be with him anymore. I pause, not sure if I should continue to read it. The Marines, sensing a 'Dear John', tell me to continue, laughing, backslapping, and commiserating with their newly single comrade. I suppose that's their way of comforting him. He manages a laugh, and seems upbeat later on. Perhaps it worked.

FRIDAY 4 JULY

On the way back to Kabul. Had a great time with the Marines, and I think I have definitely sweated off a pound or two. Going on leave in a few weeks, and I want to look good! Begin a workout routine with Dan, running ourselves to the brink of vomiting on a daily basis, followed by lifting weights until our arms shake. Oh, the things that men do to attract females.

THURSDAY 10 JULY

Just heard from Mel, who is away on an embed in the east with US forces. Their small combat outpost has been attacked by the Taliban. Instant flare of jealousy—my quest for action has fallen short, and now both Dan and Mel have had some? It doesn't feel fair. I am happy for Mel though, she sounds like she is finding her time with the American troops worthwhile.

THURSDAY 31 JULY

Watch the mountains encircling Kabul shrink below me as the Denmark-bound plane gains in altitude. Heading home for my first chunk of leave. It has been a fascinating, yet ultimately disappointing, four months. I have had an adventure, but not the excitement that I crave. I realize that most normal people would call me crazy for this nigh-on obsession with seeking combat, but I still feel it is something that I feel I need to experience. I am sure my time will come, but for now, I have a few weeks of drinking, partying, and chasing girls ahead of me. Afghanistan will still be here when I get back.

4 Empty

20 August 2008—31 December 2008

WEDNESDAY 20 AUGUST

The goodbyes are getting easier. Saying farewell to Mum and Dad—who drop me at the airport—is definitely less painful for both parties this time round. It's been an unremarkable few weeks on leave. Played up to the 'just back from a warzone' mantle, and used it for all it was worth. Met up with girls. Got drunk. Looked forward to getting back to Afghanistan. Now I'm heading back down to Helmand again to try my luck with the Danish soldiers in the Gereshk district.

THURSDAY 21 AUGUST

Land in Kabul. Round two.

FRIDAY 29 AUGUST

Arrive in Camp Bastion, the largest base in Helmand, home of several thousand British troops, and a handful of other nations—Estonians, Danes, and Americans. I walk over to Camp Viking—appropriately enough, the Danish area. I'm heading off to Gereshk tomorrow morning.

SATURDAY 30 AUGUST

5.00 a.m.—Night still has its clutches on the sky as we meet by the large Danish flag in the centre of Camp Viking. We—some Danish soldiers and myself—will be traveling to Gereshk by road. It's only an hour's drive away from Bastion, and is situated on the ring road that circles the entire country, Highway One. I am in the back of a large armoured vehicle, clanking along on heavy treads. Can barely hear myself think. Sitting with two Paras, who are also on their way to Gereshk. It's interesting to note that their knee-jerk reaction to me is different to the one I received from the Paras in April. I have ditched my pillowcase body armour, in favour of a slicker, smaller, black plate carrier which I am fervently hoping looks cooler. I have also been in country for four months, which means that I am not totally green anymore.

8.00 a.m.—Well, it's supposed to be an hour's drive, but the military runs on its own schedule. There is a suspected IED on the route, and we have to wait until it is clear to complete our journey.

When we finally arrive, I am given a brief by one of the intelligence officers. There is a fairly significant Taliban presence to the north and south of Gereshk, but the town itself—barring the odd suicide bombing— has been fairly quiet. I ask if I can get to a patrol base further north, where some Danish forces are involved in fighting. The answer is a promising 'perhaps'.

MONDAY 1 SEPTEMBER

Travelling up to FOB Sandford today, a base just a few kilometres north of Gereshk town. The Danes there have been subjected to intermittent attacks from the Taliban. I sit in a British vehicle as we wind our way slowly on the narrow paths, past the claustrophobic walls, and through the overgrown thickets of the Green Zone. There have been several IED attacks on vehicles traveling from and to Sandford, but I try not to think about it. As a passenger, watching out of the window as Helmand life goes by, there is not too much that I can do either way. Pretend to myself that I am on a pleasant Sunday drive in somewhere rural and friendly. Yeah, right.

1.00 p.m.—Arrive at Sandford. It is a sparse Hesco square—the sort that I'm becoming accustomed to seeing in this country—with a few shaded tents and a dilapidated Afghan hut in the middle. Some soldiers huddle around a laptop, laughing at a film they are watching. An enthusiastic Danish captain, Marcus, walks over and shakes my hand. Some of them are about to head out on patrol into the Green Zone. I ask if I can come along. Marcus is all too pleased to oblige, he wants to show off a well that he has commissioned some Afghan builders to construct for the local people. Hearts and minds. Get a text from Will, who is in the eastern part of Afghanistan with French troops. He is about to do several days patrolling with them and, like me, he is eagerly pursuing his first slice of action. I feel rather smug, since I fancy my chances of beating him to it—I am in the notorious Helmand, about to go into the Green Zone, after all.

We step off into the vegetation. Visibility is limited here. It's almost harvest, and therefore the fields are in their prime, with crops standing at head height. The Danish soldiers tell me that this is a double-edged sword—the Taliban can't see them, but they can't see the Taliban either. There have been incidents in the past when the insurgents have been able to get within a few meters of the soldiers and open fire, using the concealment that the crops bring. Trudging through the tall grass, with the sun blazing down on me, reminds me of a scene from *Jurassic Park*.

An Afghan interpreter (interpreters are universally nicknamed 'terps' by the soldiers), walks beside us, carrying a walkie-talkie tuned to the frequencies that the Taliban are known to use. It fascinates me that the soldiers can actually listen to the Taliban talking to each other.

'What sort of things do they say?' I ask.

'Sometimes they ask each other how they are,' the terp answers, 'other times they report that they can see us. They know that we can hear them, so they speak in code. Sometimes they will say something like 'Bring the two melons', which means "Bring the two rockets here".'

They also, apparently, try to egg each other on to be the first one to engage the ISAF forces. It reminds me of a group of kids faced with a scary situation—each one is too scared to be the first one to attempt it, and they try to encourage each other to take the plunge, hoping that somebody will initiate it.

We make our way over precarious wooden footbridges, through canals, and alongside compounds. We eventually reach the well. It's essentially a metal tube with a handle, which locals can vigorously pump to draw out water. Marcus hands a wad of cash over to the Afghan builders who have congregated proudly around their creation. We walk back to base. No sign of the Taliban.

As I remove my sweaty body armour and helmet, there are distant 'crumps' and 'booms' a few kilometres away. 'That'll be FOB Armadillo in their daily Taliban attack', a Danish soldier tells me, 'they get attacked pretty regularly.' I wish I had known about Armadillo sooner. Needless to say it is not possible to get up there: convoys seldom run, due to the IED threat. I am beginning to see a depressing pattern emerge here. The bubble endures.

FRIDAY 5 SEPTEMBER

Back in Bastion at Camp Viking, waiting for a flight back to Kabul. A few more peaceful patrols with the Danish this week, but nothing of note to report. The friendliness of the locals was a refreshing sight though, compared with the slightly hostile looks troops on patrol in Helmand receive. I was supposed to fly back to Kabul last night, but the convoy back from Gereshk was delayed by an hour, which resulted in the Hercules aircraft taking off without me. No flights today; I am hoping for one tomorrow. Spending my time sitting in a rather hot tent just waiting.

SATURDAY 6 SEPTEMBER

I am told by a Danish air movements officer that they are unable to get me on today's flight. Will try again tomorrow. Sitting here watching the clock is becoming quite draining.

SUNDAY 7 SEPTEMBER

Another 'no flight day'. Frustrated. Lie in my bed, sweating. Text from Will, which reads: 'TIC BABY!' 'TIC' means 'troops in contact'. Will has just broken his combat duck and, knowing him, he has probably got some gorgeous shots while he's at it. Instantly jealous, even more so than I was with Dan or Mel. Will and I have become very close, and with that has come a very cordial rivalry. I call him, he sounds calm, detached, different. We talk about the firefight. French troops, with Will in tow, launched an operation to clear a small village of Taliban, who fought back. NATO are ecstatic with his footage, and are looking to distribute it to French media. I spend most of the night listening to the mocking drone of the tent's faulty air conditioning unit. So frustrated.

THURSDAY 11 SEPTEMBER

10.00 p.m.—Finally get back to Kabul. Flight after flight delayed and cancelled for almost a week. It's a peculiar mental state that settles on a man after six days of near isolation. Being a fairly shy person in a tent full of Danes, I passed the week without any significant interactions. The only conversation of note was with a Danish Army psychologist—they fly him and his team here every time a Danish loss is sustained. His job is to talk to the comrades of the fallen, and try to help them through their loss. Must be a tough job, coming in to speak to combat hardened soldiers as the 'outsider', who has not shared their danger. I did not envy him.

Spent part of the flight thinking about the significance of this date, September 11. Seven years ago today, I was boarding a bus to come home from school when I heard about the attack on the World Trade Center. I dashed home to watch, in horror, the unfolding destruction on TV. As a 16-year-old schoolboy, I had no idea how much my life was going to change as a result of these events.

Trudge back to the Danish NSE from the air terminal, carrying my bags. It's good to see the team again. Ask Will to see his footage. As suspected, it is brilliant.

FRIDAY 12 SEPTEMBER

Speak to Dan on the Internet. He left the job last month to pursue other opportunities. Despite his comparatively short time with us, the experience he had in Kandahar will stay with him forever, and he is firmly embedded into the small but growing canon of NATO TV legend. There are rumours that NATO are going to employ him for a trip to the anti-piracy operation in Somalia.

MONDAY 23 SEPTEMBER

A brief change of pace for me over the next few days. Having focused on Helmand in my last few embeds, I am briefly going to the western province of Herat to spend some time with the Italian troops there. I am not sure what to make of our European allies; the Italian pilots I see walking around camp are adorned with hair gel, sunglasses, and tight flight suits.

5.00 p.m.—The Italian Hercules aircraft touches down in Herat. I am ushered into a white armoured car, where two Italian soldiers—complete with the seemingly obligatory hair product and shades—proceed to drive me through the city to the Italian base. Once again, I am struck by the completely fragmented nature of this country. Herat is modern, by Afghan standards. I see brightly coloured shops, billboards, bustling people, and even a park with a football pitch. We do not wear helmets as we travel—Helmand once again seems like a distant planet.

We arrive at the base. It is an ornate building, surrounded by paved paths and small gardens. I am led to my room—which boasts a real bed (with imitation gold bedposts), a large revolving fan, and an en suite bathroom. Absolutely mad. The Italians here are living in luxury. I go down to dinner. There are large lobsters and cartons of red wine on offer. Reminded of the squalor that the US Marines, Brits, and Danish front-line troops are currently enduring down south, I begin to feel resentful of the denizens of this camp.

TUESDAY 24 SEPTEMBER

The Italians take me to see some of the reconstruction projects in the city. There is a school, a clinic, and a prison. I dutifully film them, without much passion.

THURSDAY 26 SEPTEMBER

Fly back to Kabul. Despite the comfortable accommodation and lavish food, I am not keen to go to Herat again. It's not the war experience I am looking for. Remind myself that I work for NATO, and I must go where they want me to go.

WEDNESDAY 8 OCTOBER

My month in Europe is fast approaching, and I am desperate to try and get in some action before I go. There is now some ribbing from the rest of the team coming my way for my bad luck so far. I try to be good-natured and laugh it off, while seething inwardly. I am feeling pretty discontented right now. I haven't read my Bible in weeks, and I am glad that there is no chapel here on this base, as far as I know—it gives me an excuse not to bother trying to attend one—and I don't really feel like trying to find out whether there is one. I feel like God is punishing me right now, and I am in no way inclined to talk to or think about him.

SATURDAY 11 OCTOBER

An opportunity. The ISAF Mobile Public Affairs Team—known as MPATs—who are essentially soldiers with cameras, are heading down to Helmand for an Afghan Army operation to help to stabilize the provincial capital, Lashkar Gar. I am tasked to go with them. Compared to my usual way of operating, going along with a four-man team seems a tad cumbersome, but at this stage, I will take what I can get.

SUNDAY 12 OCTOBER

We fly down to Camp Bastion, and head over to the Afghan National Army area, Camp Shorabak, which is tacked on to the northern part of the ever-expanding Bastion. The British Operational Mentoring Liaison Team (known as OMLT—pronounced 'omelette' for the sake of ease)—a small team of soldiers that work with and train their Afghan counterparts—invite us into their HQ. Unfortunately, it seems that this trip has already become somewhat of a lame duck. The Afghans, who are supposed to be planning the operation, haven't done a very good job, and everything is quite disorganized. As far as the OMLT can tell, there isn't going to be much of an operation. Faced with disappointment after disappointment, I am fast becoming quite cynical about any attempted action that I try to put my hand to, and thus can hardly muster surprise at the news. I decide to wait around at the OMLT camp for a few days, to see if anything comes up. My time here becomes another Bastion waiting game. Joy.

MONDAY 13 OCTOBER

The OMLT headquarters is fascinating. It's my first visit inside a HQ of any type in Helmand. There is a large screen in one corner of the room, where text updates of incidents in the field are being relayed in real time. It's like watching a macabre version of the football results show in a Saturday afternoon back home, but instead of seeing something like 'Manchester United 1—0 Chelsea', you see 'IED at Checkpoint 42, 1 LN [local national—an Afghan civilian] killed, 2 ISAF injured'. It's amazing to see just how much actually goes on here that we don't hear about in the news.

TUESDAY 14 OCTOBER

It looks like things are 'nothing doing', as far as the ANA's part in this operation is concerned. The MPAT lieutenant decides to book us a helicopter to go to another base in Helmand. As I board the noisy Chinook, I am not immediately sure about where we are supposed to be going, or what we are supposed to be filming. I am told that the Chinook is making several stops, and I resolve to get off wherever we arrive first. Being in a four-man team isn't going to get me anywhere, I suspect, so I am better off splitting from them and making my own way.

The Chinook swoops low over a heavily built-up area. I can see buildings and alleyways forming a series of dusty mazes, and know this must be Lashkar Gar, the only city in Helmand. Seeing that there is an operation, albeit without the support of the Afghan National elements, taking place here, alighting at this destination is probably as good as any. The helicopter lands, I turn and mouth 'bye!' to the MPAT lieutenant, and run off the ramp of the Chinook.

I am inside the camp that frontline troops have christened 'Lash Vegas'—due to its superior food, excellent welfare facilities, and relative safety. I blunder around, trying to work out how to find a press officer, and notice there are lots of Royal Marines around: it looks like the last elements of the Para Battlegroup have finally departed Helmand. I finally find a Royal Marine captain, who works in the media department. He is slightly surprised to find me turning up like this, but I explain the situation, and he promises to see what he can do. The operation, the details of which I knew little about, turns out to be an effort to repel a sustained Taliban attack on the capital. There have been nightly gunfights, as well as several bombs. From where I am, the faint clatter of distant gunfire can be heard. I am put in a tent, and told to wait around to see what can be done to get me out there.

WEDNESDAY 15 OCTOBER

10.00 a.m.—Walk over to the media container. No luck with getting me out today. I am going to have to find some way to pass the day. Fortunately, I am becoming quite an expert at waiting.

11.00 p.m.—Lying in the tent. There is a distant, deep 'pop'. A second of silence, followed by the horrific clichéd whistling of an incoming shell. It's the closest I have ever heard. The disconcertingly cinematic wail intensifies, telegraphing a visceral sense of speed, mass and immediate violence. Unable to do much, I roll off my bed onto the floor and hope for the best. It slams into the earth just outside camp with a noise like ground-level thunder. The siren sounds. There are no cupboards to hide in here, and that last shot sounded horribly close, so I dutifully make my way to the shelter to wait out the hours with the other bleary-eyed people for several uneventful hours.

THURSDAY 16 OCTOBER

The Marines are unable to get me out to the checkpoints that I need to pass, and the operation seems to be winding up without me. It's time to head back to Kabul, once again, with my tail between my legs. I am now beginning to firmly believe that it is some sort of cruel fate intended for me to always miss out on the one thing I am trying to get. It's my Europe stint in two weeks, very disappointed.

FRIDAY 31 OCTOBER

Arrived in Copenhagen, Denmark, late last night. I will be staying here for a month or so, working out of the Danish Defence Media Center (FMC), covering any stories NATO have in Europe. As far as I know, there aren't any plans for me to do anything.

WEDNESDAY 5 NOVEMBER

Spent the weekend sitting in the flat the FMC have provided for us, drinking and watching James Bond films. Being in an unfamiliar city, I suppose that I should be out enjoying the sights and sounds of Copenhagen, but I feel completely empty and unmotivated. I am lower than I can remember being for years. During the week, I complete my hours at the FMC, then return to the flat to resume my drinking and Bond movies. I try to tell myself that I am just down because of my run of bad luck this far in Afghanistan, and that things will look up. I don't find this as convincing as I once did, though. I am further from God than I think I have ever been in my life, and I know that it should really bother me. Again, however, it only registers as a faint sense of guilt stirred into my self-pity.

MONDAY 10 NOVEMBER

Mel emails me from Kabul. Will has got malaria. At first, she thought he was suffering from 'man flu', and repeatedly told him to 'man up', but upon entering his room to see him covered in sweat, and having a fevered conversation with 'Josh'—despite the fact that I was in another country—she realized that he was really suffering. Thomas, our boss, springs into action and prepares to get Will flown out of Afghanistan so that he can recover.

WEDNESDAY 12 NOVEMBER

Go to the airport with Dan—briefly in Copenhagen after his stint on the Somali coast—to meet the pale, thin-looking Will. He slaps us away as we playfully offer him a wheelchair. Such sympathy. We put him on a flight back to the UK.

THURSDAY 4 DECEMBER

A completely unremarkable month in Denmark. Sitting in Copenhagen airport, waiting to check in for the now-familiar flight back to Afghanistan, I watch as Danish soldiers arrive in dribs and drabs with tearful families in tow. A father holds his little son close as his wife watches them, biting her lip. A young, blonde guy clutches his equally blonde girlfriend in the final, bitter moments of parting. These men are headed to Helmand, and it's not guaranteed that they will all come home. Those that do may bear scars that they will carry for the rest of their lives. I sit and watch, an outsider, already in one foreign land, and about to head into an exponentially more alien one. I am glad that I don't have to do any goodbyes.

FRIDAY 5 DECEMBER

Arrive in Kabul, and am immediately on the go. Michael, a Danish major briefly filling in for Kristian, wants to drive with me to Kapisa—a district several hours drive north of Kabul. The taxi option is not viable: 'KH', our Afghan taxi boss, has gone missing, and we suspect he has been taken by the NDS, the Afghan equivalent of the CIA. We are not sure why. His drivers still give us rides occasionally, but either way, it wouldn't be a good idea to get a taxi to this remote area.

The French Foreign Legion who are stationed there are expecting us. I am intrigued—most people have heard of the Legion and their fearsome reputation—but to my shame I am finding myself becoming increasingly bitter towards the nations which are not engaged in the heavy fighting that the British, Americans, and Canadians are shouldering. The French, to be fair, did recently lose ten men in a horrific Taliban ambush.

12 p.m.—Set off with Michael. The drive is expected to take two or three hours. Before long, we are out of the Kabul city limits, and winding our way through the snow-powdered cracks between the towering mountains. The only weapons we have in the car are Michael's M4 rifle, a pistol, and some smoke grenades. I fervently hope that the Taliban have shut up shop for the winter, and that we won't be caught or killed. The images of the Taliban parading the uniforms of the slaughtered French soldiers replay in my mind as we pass through the country.

4.00 p.m.—We finally arrive at the French camp, due to some impressive map reading from Michael. There was a delay, however, when an Afghan on a motorbike fell off and hurt himself several hundred meters ahead of us. We stopped the car, jumped out, and made sure he wasn't too seriously injured before driving away quickly. Word spreads quickly here, and we didn't want it known that two Westerners were hanging around in a remote area.

It is bitterly cold up here. Foreign Legion soldiers walk around, faces wrapped in scarves as the wind howls around them, and I am glad I am not based up here. It is cheerless.

SATURDAY 6 DECEMBER

There's not a wealth of material to film here, unfortunately. The Legion are not patrolling during our stay, so we have to make do with filming on base, which is never an overly stimulating experience. I interview some Legionaries—some of whom give false names, no doubt to cover their dubious pasts—and two American helicopters turn up to do a missile demonstration, bathing one side of a nearby mountain in fire and shrapnel.

SUNDAY 7 DECEMBER

The way the French do breakfast confuses me. I understand that they enjoy their light 'bread, milk, jam, and croissant' continental breakfast, but as an Englishman, used to hearty, warm fare (even if it is processed gloop out of a ration pack) I cannot see how they can enjoy stale, cold bread in sub-zero temperatures. It might be nice on a sunny Parisian morning, but out here it is downright depressing. Give me processed baked beans any day.

1.00 p.m.—Drive back to Kabul with Michael, a thankfully uneventful trip. We turn the car's heating up to the max.

MONDAY 8 DECEMBER

Mel, despite the teasing she gives me about my bubble of bad luck, is beginning to feel sorry for me. She has set up an embed for me with the Canadians down in Kandahar. They lost their one-hundredth soldier in combat while I was with the French.

Reaching such a poignant number is sobering. I had the misfortune of being in Iraq when the British death toll reached one hundred, and again in Afghanistan during the summer a similarly unwanted milestone was marked.

WEDNESDAY 10 DECEMBER

Arrive in KAF. Sick of KAF. Thankfully only here for a few hours, before heading into Kandahar city itself, to Camp Nathan Smith—one of the primary Canadian bases here. Each nation that I have spent time with has different ways of acting in potentially dangerous territory, and the Canadians are the most cautious, stopping to extensively check every culvert and ditch for IEDs. This could turn a three-mile journey into a six-hour affair. The Americans and Danes, by contrast, would often just go for it. It's hard to say which method was better. To use a particularly brutal strain of logic, I suppose your viewpoint on the issue depends on whether you're the one to get blown up or not.

Finally arrive at Camp Nathan Smith, called 'CNS' by its inhabitants. I immediately suspect that I have been given the softer, flabbier end of the Canadian war effort. There is fresh fruit, good internet, and even a swimming pool. A swimming pool, in Afghanistan. Speechless. Prepare myself to spend the next few days filming positive, but ultimately uninteresting reconstruction-based stories. Gargh.

FRIDAY 12 DECEMBER

3.00 p.m.—See some Canadian soldiers rushing to their vehicles. I ask the Canadian press officer what is happening. He tells me that there is some sort of IED find in the city, and that they are going to deal with it. Interesting. 'Can I go with them?' I ask. He runs over and asks their commander, who agrees on the condition that the press officer accompanies me. Fine by me. We head out into the city.

4.00 p.m.—We arrive at the suspected IED location. The suspected bomb is right outside an Afghan Army base, and is in a large plastic bag on the back of a bicycle. Afghan soldiers and police have already cordoned off the area—an impressive display of professionalism from our often chaotic allies—and are waiting for the Canadian bomb-disposal team. Apparently, a young male cycled the bike up next to the base, leant it against a shop pillar, and promptly ran off. An inquisitive Afghan soldier had a peek in the bag, and was startled to see a rather large bomb. A Canadian bomb disposal expert, who calls himself 'John' (although I suspect this is an alias), carefully guides a remote control robot up to the bike.

On the roof of a building about two hundred meters away, and on the other side of the cordoned off area from the troops, a head keeps popping up and down, watching the unfolding scene, then hiding again. 'That could be the trigger man,' a Canadian soldier tells me. 'He could be waiting until somebody gets close to it, then he'll detonate. He could also just be an interested local.' A very difficult situation.

Light is beginning to fade—sunset in Afghanistan is never much later than 6 p.m.—and in the winter months it is even earlier. We have been here for over an hour now, watching the painstaking process play out.

The robot is unable to determine exactly what manner of bomb it is, and attempts at remote deactivation fail, so John decides to put on his Kevlar suit and take what is known as 'the long walk' toward the device. I crouch behind a vehicle and film him as he walks. Even after all my thirst for action, I would not want to be him right now. Glance over at the roof—the head hasn't appeared for a while now. Is that a good or a bad thing? John reaches the device. There is a collective intake of breath from Canadian troops, Afghan soldiers, and Afghan police alike as he carefully crouches over the bomb. Time becomes horribly viscous as we watch. After what seems like an eternity, he turns and gives the thumbs up. Bomb deactivated. John removes several parts from the device which will be used for evidence, and I am allowed to film what is left.

Every day, all over Afghanistan, and particularly in the south, men like John take 'the long walk' again and again. Some survive, others don't. Inspirational.

WEDNESDAY 17 DECEMBER

After a few days of patrolling with the Canadians, I head back to Kabul. I'd rather not spend Christmas in KAF. I resolve, as much as is in my power, not to see this airfield for some time. It's just utterly soulless.

THURSDAY 25 DECEMBER

Christmas in Kabul. Mel and I have volunteered to be the poor saps who stay in country over the festive period. David is with his long-term girlfriend, and Will is on a post-malaria holiday in Thailand. I spend the day drinking and watching *The Lord of the Rings* films, and trying to fix a remote helicopter that mum sent me as a gift.

WEDNESDAY 31 DECEMBER

The Danes at the NSE invite us for a New Year's Eve dinner. There is some very strong alcohol involved. I drink far too much, and spend most of the night curled over the toilet, vomiting. In between bouts of nausea, I reflect murkily on 2008. One year ago, I think, I felt completely down and out, and then, out of nowhere, I landed this amazing job. I catch myself thinking this. At the time of getting this job, it was God that I was grateful to, not myself. That seems so long ago. I feel like I have barely spoken to God seriously for most of the year; compared to how I am now, even last winter's misery seems like a spiritual high point. I feel utterly empty, unsatisfied, hollow. I don't even know if the root of this is the lack of action, this increasingly nebulous thing I crave. I suspect that it isn't. These thoughts echo in my mind as I fall asleep, head spinning, feeling sick. Happy new year.

5 Prodigal

3 January 2009—23 February 2009

SATURDAY 3 JANUARY

Flurries of snow sweep down on Kabul. It seems that we narrowly missed a very white Christmas indeed. I have tried to put the thoughts of New Year's Eve out of my head, and brace myself for the potential adventures that 2009 has to offer. Sadly, it doesn't seem to be holding much promise thus far.

TUESDAY 13 JANUARY

I draw the short straw, and am sent on a trip to Herat with two NATO staff, to film a story about a wireless Internet service that is being installed in Herat university. Riveting. The NATO staff are obviously very excited about it, it's their baby, but I am nurturing a rather bad attitude. To me, it's a boring story in a place I already dislike. We spend the night at the Italian 'hotel' base that I was in last year.

THURSDAY 15 JANUARY

Bad weather forces us to wait in Herat longer than expected. I filmed the story yesterday, and will have to edit when I return to Kabul. I suspect that the NATO staff have noticed my attitude, but in my mind it serves them right for dragging me on this non-story. The faint whisperings of conscience are lost on me.

MONDAY 26 JANUARY

David and Will are now back, and it's good to be a family again. We have all become very close over the past year. This will be David's last stint in Afghanistan; a year away from his long-term girlfriend Laura is trial enough, and he will now be taking up the European posting full-time. I am secretly very grateful for this—I hate the idea of filming NATO stories in Europe, far away from where the war is, and am glad he will be willingly shouldering the burden. At the same time, I have never been in a long-term relationship before, and privately I have little empathy for David and Laura's situation—for me, it's all about the Afghan experience. In any case, I will be sad to see him go.

WEDNESDAY 4 FEBRUARY

2.00 p.m.—Gunfire in town today. I jump in a taxi—KH is still in the hands of the NDS, but Ahmad is still a great help in getting around town—and ask Ahmad to take me to where the fighting is taking place. Excitement surges through me as we park the taxi, and begin to run toward where we can hear the shooting. Ahmad trails reluctantly behind me. He probably didn't imagine this when I asked if he could be my translator today. Gunfire is coming from one of the Afghan Government buildings—the Ministry of Justice. We reach a police cordon. Despite my ISAF ID, which I wave around frantically, they refuse to let me through; it is too dangerous. Ahmad asks them what is happening. They tell us that the Taliban have attacked the Ministry, and have killed several Government officials. They are now making a desperate last stand in the upper offices as US Special Forces and Afghan Commandos storm the building.

Frustrated at not being able to get any closer, Ahmad and I dash several hundred meters to try and get near the building from another angle. There is already a media scrum there—a mix of local and international press—who are being held at another cordon. We are told that one of the first arrivals on the scene, a local Afghan cameraman, strayed too close to the building and was shot by one of the Taliban, who seem simply to want to kill as many people as they can before they are finally taken out.

The gunfire subsides, and we get reports that the building is clear. After a few minutes, some thickly built, heavily bearded white guys in sunglasses come out. A battered Humvee screeches up beside them, and they jump in. Every red blooded male present looks at them longingly; they are super-cool, the pinnacle of manhood, elite soldiers. An enterprising Afghan cameraman runs up to the Humvee to get a close-up shot of these mysterious soldiers and one of them, a man with a large brown beard, hurls a full water bottle into the unfortunate Afghan's face at point blank range. The cameraman hits the floor, lesson learned: film Special Forces at your peril.

MONDAY 23 FEBRUARY

My birthday. Twenty-four years old. I spent my twenty-first birthday in Iraq, and now this one in Afghanistan. I think back over this year of my life. In some ways, I don't recognize what I have become. I drink, regularly and heavily, I swear, using words that I never thought I'd ever say, I chase girls, I am selfish, easily jealous, and in a big, big mess. Josh, the pastor's son, the churchgoer, the Christian, seems like somebody else in the distant past. I feel like a husk at the moment, desperately hoping for combat, seeking the glory and the respect from other people that comes with it. Enough is enough. I can't live like this anymore. I don't want to be this person for a moment longer.

It takes me a while to find my camouflage Bible; it is gathering dust beneath my bed. I don't even feel worthy to open it. I have horrendously turned my back on God in the last year, and crawling back to him now is a humbling experience. 'Lord,' I whisper out loud, 'I don't even know what to say, apart from this: I am so, so sorry. You have given me this amazing job, wonderful friends, and incredible experiences, and yet I have rejected you. I have made the pursuit of combat and glory my number one goal in life, and I have forgotten you. I am truly, deeply, sorry. I need your forgiveness for the things that I have done, and right now I want to make you my focus. I will no longer chase combat—I will trust in you. I believe that you are in control of everything, and that you know what is best for me in life. Amen.'

I open my Bible and begin to read; it's the story that Jesus told about the prodigal son, a man that spurns his father's love and squanders his inheritance in a selfish lifestyle, but then comes crawling back, broken, poor, and depressed. The father, instead of being angry with his son, welcomes him back with open arms and great love. Jesus told this story to demonstrate just how much God loves us, despite the way that we treat him. I have known this story since I was a boy, but never have I appreciated it more. I go to sleep, truly at peace for the first time in a year; my future is in God's hands.

6 Contact

27 February 2009—10 March 2009

FRIDAY 27 MARCH

The British in Helmand have invited me down for an embed with the Estonian soldiers serving there. I didn't even know that there were Estonians in Helmand. Usually, I would begin to desperately hope for combat—but this time it is different. I am leaving it all to God. I will just do the best I can, and let him take care of the rest.

SUNDAY 1 MARCH

Fly down to Helmand (once again). Think I've been on over fifty flights so far in this job. Arrive in Camp Bastion. Met by a British Royal Marine press officer, who drops me off at the Estonian camp.

The camp—more like a small compound—looks fairly sparse. Not sure what to think. A lonely Estonian flag flutters meekly in the breeze. I am given odd looks by passing soldiers. Need to find someone in charge. Out of a nearby hut a small blonde man appears.

'Are you the NATO camera guy?' he asks in halting English. Once again, slightly embarrassed that I am only able to speak English, still unable to meet the citizens of other countries on their level, I reply, 'Yes'.

He introduces himself as Maart, and takes me on a brief tour of the camp. He is in charge of keeping the Estonian soldiers logistically supplied, and seems slightly irritated that reporters only ever want to focus on the 'action'. I sympathize with him, and assure him that I will cover his efforts during my visit.

He introduces me to the Estonian company commander, Raigo, who briefs me about the upcoming operation that I am to take part in. We will be conducting a 'surge operation', launching forward into an area dominated by the Taliban with the intent of pushing them back. Despite the cynical voice in my head, this actually does look quite promising. The problem is that I have just under a week to kill until it kicks off. Oh well, I've waited long enough for something like this, six days is just a drop in the ocean.

MONDAY 2 MARCH

Go for a run around Bastion. Halfway round, a truckload of Estonian soldiers drives past. I can see that they recognize me as the guy who has been loitering around their camp holding a camera. I transform my face to look focused, intense. Anything but exhausted. Must look competent. The truck disappears into the distance, and I allow myself to become a panting heap.

WEDNESDAY 4 MARCH

2.00 a.m.—Get up. Not even sure if it even counts as 'getting up' when it's this early. Driving in a convoy down to a place called Nawa to re-supply British unit there. I think the plan is to go to Nawa after our surge op this weekend.

4.00 a.m.—Finally depart Bastion. I am traveling in Raigo's vehicle. I love these machines, having spent far too much time being cramped up in American Humvees and stuffy Brit vehicles. In these things, there's space! About eight meters long, and three meters wide, six wheels, lots of room. In my vehicle, as an added bonus, are a couple of British soldiers. It seems that the Brits are needed to run the radio and speak to the aircraft that are acting in support above us. It makes sense, and helps to negotiate the potentially dangerous language barrier between the British and Estonian forces in Helmand. I am sitting beside Neil, a commando attached to the Estonians as a JTAC (Joint Terminal Air Controller). It's his job to coordinate and call in any air support if we get into a fight with the Taliban. We instantly get along—he is wearing the parachute qualification badge, something I also got in the Paras. Common ground, always a good starting point.

10.00 a.m.—Arrive in Nawa. As the crow flies, it's actually not very far away from Bastion, but because of the risk of IEDs and mines, the journey takes a good few hours. The British base here, Patrol Base Jaker, has a real frontline feel about it. Bullet holes line the walls. There's even an old artillery shell crater near the toilets, and when I say toilets, I mean 'large pipe embedded in the ground that you aim your business into'. I have just missed a large firefight with the Taliban. The soldiers here have an unkempt and slightly wild look about them. Dust lines every crevice in every weary face. We stay for a few hours, offloading hundreds of water bottles and ration-packs for the troops here. Time to go. Slightly unwillingly, I climb back into Raigo's vehicle. Can't wait to come back here next week.

Patrol Base Jaker.

THURSDAY 3 MARCH

3.00 a.m.—Finally get back to Bastion. Have never needed the toilet as much as I do now. Lots of delays on the way back, spent over twelve hours sitting in the same seat. Sleep for most of the day.

FRIDAY 4 MARCH

Surge operation begins early tomorrow morning. We receive a final brief from Raigo: we will be going into a village in the Changir Triangle, part of an area called Nad-e-Ali. Everybody seems to think that we will meet some fairly staunch Taliban resistance there. Excited.

Maart gives me some gloves, some ballistic glasses, and a red torch. I am ready. Raigo tells me to be meet at 3.00 a.m. by the vehicles. The Estonian soldiers are beginning to warm to me. This week of killing time seems to have proved beneficial in that regard at least.

8.00 p.m.—Lots of Brit vehicles preparing to go. They will be surging into a village next to where we are headed. Try to get an early night, but I'm too excited to sleep. Call my Dad, who prays with me. I even liberate a scrap of bread and some grape juice from the food tent so I can have my own mini Communion service on the eve of battle. Check, double-check, and triple-check my camera. Everything working. Lie back on my bed, and commit the next few days to God in prayer. Despite my fear, I know that he is sovereign—nothing will happen to me that is outside of his control. It's a very reassuring thing to know.

SATURDAY 7 MARCH

3.00 a.m.—Here we go. I get up, and walk through the darkness to the Estonian vehicle parking area. One by one, small points of red light get closer, as soldiers make their way over from their tents. I film them stowing their bags away.

4.00 a.m.—We depart Camp Bastion. I am suddenly very grateful for the

Nawa excursion the other day. Feel at home in this vehicle, with these guys. Exchange some banter with Neil. He got married just before he left for Afghan. I feel for his wife.

We stop in the desert, about ten minutes away from the edge of Nad-e-Ali, waiting for the first glimpse of sunrise. I climb out of the vehicle and relieve myself, not sure when I will get another chance.

After what seems like an age, we finally start moving again. The banter stops. Neil becomes focused, staring intently into a small screen he carries around with him, looking at the video feed from an American F-16 fighter jet above us, alert for any sign of the Taliban. We are all swamped in an eerie red light.

In the distance there is a crackle of gunfire, and some low thumping sounds. Jay, one of the British radio operators, listens in on the net. 'Boys, the Marines to the west of us have engaged two Taliban targets. One had an RPG (rocket propelled grenade). Both dead.' I think today is going to be the day—give me courage for what I need to do, Lord.

7.00 a.m.—We arrive at a large scrapyard that overlooks our objective—a small village we will be pushing into later on. Estonian soldiers immediately begin to clear as much of the metal away from us as they can. A Taliban rocket in the middle of this place would create a starburst of deadly shrapnel. We are all starving, so during the clearing operation we dig greedily and deeply into our foil-packed rations. You know you are hungry when those things taste good. Two other commandos from another vehicle, Rob and Pete, join Neil. We instantly click. I like these guys, my small slice of British normality amongst the flood of Estonians. Raigo calls us all together and gives us a final brief. Rob and Pete, with a platoon of Estonian soldiers, will head up the right-hand side of the village. They will stop and give the other Estonian platoon— who will be moving up the centre of the village—any fire support they need. Raigo asks me which platoon I'd like to go with: second platoon, on the right hand side of the village, or first platoon, going up the middle. I hate choices at the best of times. So scarred am I by my perceived bad luck thus far that I assume that whoever I choose won't get any action. I try to ignore these feelings, and choose first platoon. No such thing as luck, Josh! Trust in God!

12.00 noon—Second platoon head off. Pete grins at me: 'See you on the other side, mate.' It takes well over an hour for second platoon to get where they need to go. The rest of us take cover behind a large bank, which overlooks the village. Neil chatters away to the pilots above us, continuing his vigil for any sign of the Taliban. We hear that women and children are exiting out the back end of the village. This usually means that they are expecting a fight. Excited. Peek over the bank at the village. There is an odd glittering flash on the rooftop of one of the houses. Flash. Flash. Flash. 'Taliban using mirrors to signal to each other,' Raigo tells me.

2.00 p.m.—It's very hot. Sitting here with my camera in my lap, waiting for something to happen. Will anything happen though? It's been quiet for a while now. Eyes begin to close. Very tired after the journey last night. Suddenly there is a whizzing sound above me. Was that a bullet?! Estonian

In the village, trying not to let my fear show.

soldiers around me hunker down in cover. Off to our right, gunfire suddenly erupts. It sounds like Rob, Pete, and second platoon are under attack. I curse my decision—why did I pick first platoon?! The gunfire continues for about half an hour. I hope Rob and Pete are ok. Neil coordinates with an Apache attack helicopter above us. It buzzes angrily as it unleashes a salvo of fire on the Taliban positions. A terrifying sight.

News comes through that there is an injury—an Afghan policeman has been shot in the leg. He is brought back to where we are, and a medevac (medical evacuation) helicopter is called for. Before long, I can hear the dull 'whumph' of its rotors as it draws near. Encouraging. If I get shot, at least they will pick me up fairly quickly. The Afghan policeman is helped aboard, and the helicopter departs for Camp Bastion. Raigo tells me to get ready. It is time to enter the village.

3.00 p.m.—Kajaar, the first platoon commander, slots me into the formation just behind him. Quite near the back. Hope I will still be able to get some good footage if this kicks off. We walk slowly into the village, in a staggered column, walking down the main path. Everything is deadly quiet. CRACK! CRACK! CRACK! Suddenly the air is alive with bullets, and they are aimed at us. CRACK! CRACK! I have heard about the infamous 'cracks' from combat veterans, but had never imagined how terrifying they would be. It sounds like some great whip snapping in my ear. Press record button on the camera. CRACK! These bullets are close. The Estonians at the front of the column are quick to react, jumping on their bellies and returning fire. I crouch behind Kajaar as he assesses the situation. A million thoughts are running through my head. CRACK! CRACK! 'Let's go! Stick with me!' Kajaar shouts, and begins to make his way up to the front. I am split. Very happy to be making my way towards some cover, but not happy about the idea of running towards people who are trying to kill me. It takes every ounce of will I have to force my legs to follow him. I am not a brave person by nature; I am scared of the ball hitting me when I play football. CRACK! That was close. Really close. JesusJesusJesus. I am praying as I run, the word 'Jesus' being the only word I am able to articulate. CRACK! CRACK! Take cover behind the corner of a house with Kajaar and a few other Estonians. So this is what it

Tonis bandages the wound on his leg.

feels like. My heart is pumping. I have never felt this alive in my whole life. I want to cry—not out of fear, but out of sheer exhilaration. Kajaar sends some soldiers through the house in a bid to flank the Taliban. I am left with a handful of soldiers, who continue to trade fire with the Taliban.

Over to our left, three soldiers, who are in an alleyway, begin to yell. I don't understand them, but they look panicked. Kajaar bellows to the machine gunner on the floor, who begins putting down a heavy weight of fire at the Taliban position. The three soldiers run over to us. One has been shot in the leg, the other in the chest-plate of his armour. It appears that the Taliban had the same flanking idea that Kajaar did. The guy who has been shot in the leg is a medic named Tonis. He sits down painfully. There are not many hands free, so I decide to help him. Forget 'pack to da bone', he will probably hit me if I jam my fingers in his wound. Revert to bandaging technique I learned in the army. Hands shaking. 'Want me to do it instead?' Tonis asks. Good point. He is a medic after all, and his hands aren't hit. I let him take over, and record the process on my camera.

5.00 p.m.—The firefight is becoming more sporadic in nature. Kajaar receives orders to pull out of the village—we will need more men than just a platoon to clear this, and Neil is eager to have us out of the way so he can call in some airstrikes. Using the walls as cover, we begin to make our way out of the village. Taliban fire intensifies. CRACKCRACKCRACK! I reach the last bit of cover. Going to have to move out into the open and run like a madman to reach the bank where Neil, Raigo, and the other soldiers are. Bullets kick up dust on the path in front of me. I do not want to do this. Ergo, the Estonian engineer next to me, grins. He pats his buttocks, motioning that I should stick with him as he runs. I nod. Mouth dry with fear. Suddenly, Ergo is running. I break cover and follow him. Runningrunning runningrunning. CRACK! CRACK! CRACK! CRACK! I've never run so fast in my life. Reach the bank, throw myself over the top of it. Sweet, sweet relief. Ergo collapses next to me, panting. 'War is hell,' he says. We both burst out laughing, elated to be alive.

7.00 p.m.—After some more sporadic shooting, the Taliban finally go to

An Estonian soldier fires a rocket at the Taliban as we withdraw.

sleep for the night. Tonis has been medevac'd back to Bastion. Rob and Pete made it back an hour after Ergo and I ran to the bank. They have had similar close calls. We sit around, eating our rations, and talking about the day's events. Everyone wants to tell their story. No one is seriously injured, and it feels against all rational understanding like we have just taken part in a great, death-defying game. The sense of exhilaration after combat is incredible. Despite the fact that we have only known each other for less than a week, the instant bond that shared combat creates is fascinating; some of the soldiers can't even speak the same language as me, but it doesn't seem to matter.

I go to bed early, lying in the scrapyard, staring up at the bright moon. It has faint glowing rings around it. Beautiful. Thank you Lord for getting me through today, and giving me the strength to do what I had to. Please be with me during the rest of this operation.

SUNDAY 8 MARCH

6.00 a.m.—Wake up early. Freezing. Turns out the beautiful rings around the moon were ice crystals in the upper atmosphere, apparently. Ice on my sleeping bag. People beginning to stir into life. Wonder what today will hold?

9.00 a.m.—Raigo calls us together. We are to head to a nearby area today, to try to cut off some of the Taliban's support. Once again, he turns to me and asks who I'd like to go with. I really appreciate the way the Estonians are handling this. I choose second platoon this time—it's only fair. Neil gets attached to second platoon as well, which makes me happy—good to have a friendly face along. The platoon commander, Juri, introduces himself. He shows me a picture of his baby boy, then reverently sticks it back on the door of his vehicle. I hope nothing happens to him. We board vehicles and depart.

11.00 a.m.—Been rumbling around for a few hours now. Lots of stopping and starting. We finally halt. Radio chatter. The aircraft above us spot some men acting suspiciously. Juri dismounts, and I follow. He takes cover by a wall and begins to scan the nearby fields with his binoculars. It's spring, and the grass is already growing high in the warm sum. BANG! BANG! BANG! I jump about a foot in the air. The gunner on top our vehicle has just fired the .50 calibre machinegun at a man he saw running through the field with a weapon. .50 bullets are large. Legend has it that one merely needs to pass within a foot of your arm to rip it off. Not sure if that's true or not, but wouldn't fancy testing it out. Being in front and underneath of this weapon as it fires almost deafens me. I can feel the force of the gas being released on my cheek. As the cannon fires I hastily scurry behind the gunner. Silence. Juri can't see the man anymore.

We suddenly hear the clatter of gunfire a few hundred meters away to the right, where first platoon's vehicles are. Juri looks at the large mud brick wall of the compound that separates the platoons, and speaks rapidly to an Estonian engineer. The engineer nods, and grabs some plastic explosives from his bag. He places them against the wall about fifty meters away and lights a fuse. Everybody gets under cover. I have never seen an explosion this close before, and realise that I can't miss the opportunity to film it. I brace myself against the opposite wall about thirty meters from the fuse, which seems to be in no hurry to burn down. Am I too close? Am I going to get hit by flying stones? Should I be do- BOOOOOM! Faster than my mind can process it, a shockwave from the blast tears through the dust towards me and knocks me back. The camera and I are unharmed, but I can't see anything through the cloud of dust. When it clears, a large and astonishingly ncat hole in the wall is revealed.

Juri grabs his rifle and runs through it. I follow him, with our vehicle close behind. As he contacts Raigo, asking the best position in which to set up and provide covering fire, there is a new clattering sound, closer, louder, and coming from where we just left. Juri runs back through the hole. Not wanting to be left alone, I follow him. The remaining members of Juri's platoon are hunkered down against a sand bank, trading fire with the Taliban. We are about one hundred meters away. Open ground between the platoon and us. Juri begins to run. I pray. Here we go again. CRACK! CRACK! I drop to the ground halfway across. Lie there for a second, panting. It's really heating up. Stumble to my feet and run the remaining distance. Throw myself into the sand bank, and film the soldiers engaging the enemy with rockets, rifles, and a .50 cal. After a few minutes, Juri gets up, preparing to run back. Again? Really? Reluctantly, I follow him. CRACKCRACKCRACK! Staying as close as I can. I trip over in the open ground. Lie there for a second, trying to take cover behind a small clod of protruding earth. CRACK! Not the best idea. Haul myself to my feet and run back through the hole to Juri.

In the compound, we see Neil on top of a rooftop, trying to speed up the arrival of an Apache helicopter. We run toward him. As we get close, two big puffs of dust kick up next to his head. He ducks. Too close. We reach him. He thinks the Taliban have realised that he is linked to the threat from the air.

Before long, the reassuring, lazy buzz of the Apache can be heard as it looms into view over the battle. Taliban fire ceases immediately.

4.00 p.m.—All has been quiet since the Apache turned up. We make camp in a high-walled compound, and settle down around our vehicles in the tall grass. My shirt is sticking to me: having worn it for three days straight now, the salt from my prodigious sweat is stiffening it.

7.00 p.m.—Raigo calls the platoon commanders, Rob, and Neil into his vehicle. The rest of us wait outside, eating, resting, and joking around. Pete opens up a package that he has been saving. It's from his girlfriend's family: a pack of cigars. 'According to government research, smoking will kill you,' he reads aloud, 'but so will an RPG, so smoke on lads and keep your heads down!' We all laugh.

Raigo's brief finishes. Neil and Rob come back with the news. We are heading back to yesterday's village first thing tomorrow. This time, Raigo intends to clear it fully.

11.00 p.m.—Lying on my roll mat. Can't sleep. Have to get up in four hours to begin making our way to the village. Nerves singing with anticipation as the minutes drop past. Despite yesterday's euphoria, I can't help but feel that the Taliban won—they pushed us out. They won't be giving this village up without a fight. Someone is going to die. I look at the stars. Somewhere, thousands of miles away back home, my friends and family are meeting for the evening service at church. Here I am, not knowing if I will be alive in twelve hours. Couldn't feel further away. Dreading the 'crack' sound.

Read my Iraq psalm from my camouflage Bible, using a red torch in my sleeping bag:

'Though an army besiege me, my heart will not fear; though war break out againt me, even then I will be confident.' (Psalm 27:3)

MONDAY 9 MARCH

3.00 a.m.—Someone grabs my shoulder and gently shakes me awake. Time to go. I leap up, surprising myself. By rights I should feel sleep-gummed and groggy, but the adrenaline is already roaring through me. We pack our bags and board the vehicles in the inky pre-dawn. The journey to the village seems much quicker at night.

4.00 a.m.—We arrive in the scrapyard, quietly dismount, and assemble in our groups. I move over to Kajaar and 1 platoon—their turn to have me along for the ride again. Rob, Pete, and Raigo also join us. Neil lets us know that as yet there is no sign of any enemy activity in the village. The aim is to infiltrate in as far as possible: if all goes well, the Taliban will wake up with us on their doorsteps. Everyone speaks in hushed, focused whispers as we receive the order to move out. Here we go.

Staying off the path, creeping through the vegetation that we retreated through two days ago, we approach our target. The first faint stains of dawn are beginning to fade into the sky, the dark, sharp silhouettes of the long grass contrasting with the blue-pink of the lightening sky. Nobody makes a sound. One of the British radiomen in front of me quietly curses as his antenna is caught on a branch. I help him untangle himself as noiselessly as possible.

We reach the first compound of the village—the same compound that Kajaar and I took cover next to, where Tonis was shot. It feels odd to be able to creep up to it with impunity, without so much as a shot fired from the Taliban. Rob receives a radio message from the Estonian snipers, and relays it to Pete and I. 'Snipers on the high ground can see what looks like women and kids, leaving out the back end of the village.' It seems our progress hasn't been entirely undetected. The locals here know what is about to happen next. Pete then receives a message that men with motorbikes have been seen entering the village. The Taliban are here.

The sun appears on the horizon: brilliant, warm, golden, and entirely unconcerned with the squabbles of Helmand province. It is a beautiful morning. We press on further into the village. My blood begins to thunder quietly in my ears. The Taliban could be anywhere. It's just a matter of time until they attack us, surely. It feels intensely like one of those anxious moments in cinema when you know that the bad guy is about to strike, but can do nothing at all about it. That feeling is so much more potent when you are liable to be the target. A Taliban radio message is intercepted. 'It just came through,' says Karli, Raigo's radioman, 'they are ready in the houses for us.' Rob warns us to be switched on—the fight could start meters from us, if we are not careful. We move further.

9.00 a.m.—second platoon report that they have found a compound that has been used by the Taliban. It is full of training manuals, pictures of grenades, propaganda posters, and weapons. We stop inside another compound. The sun is fast melting away the chill in the air. It's going to be a hot one, today. We receive the order to move deeper into the village. We stand and shoulder our bags. CRACKCRACKCRACK! Suddenly the world erupts in the now-familiar cacophony of violence. 'That's incoming fire on our position,' says Rob, calmly. 'Get yourselves in some cover, boys!' Just outside the compound, Kajaar and his men are hunched behind a wall, trading fire with the Taliban. Rob and Pete crawl forward, trying to work out where the Taliban positions are so they can call in artillery support. I follow them. Kajaar sees me, comparatively out in the open, between the compound and the wall where he is. CRACK! CRACK! 'Come here come here come here!' he yells. I crawl over to the wall, turn the camera on and begin to film myself explaining the situation. BOOM! An RPG explodes nearby. A bullet knocks a chunk from a wall several meters away. An Estonian soldier cackles as he survives a near miss. Rob yells that the artillery is incoming. CRUMP-BOOM! The shells begin to slam down. Even from several hundred meters away, they produce a colossal noise. It must be nightmarish to be on the receiving end of one. More support arrives in the form of an Apache, a knight in dull green armour. It begins to immediately engage the Taliban fighters it can see.

There is a slight lull in incoming fire, and Kajaar's men take the opportunity to rush forward and clear the next set of compounds. It reminds me of a game of American football; every yard gained, every compound taken, is of critical importance. Once the compounds are secured, we all push up to them. We get reports that the Taliban are now fleeing from the village. We pause in one of the northernmost compounds and await further orders. It is close to midday now, and the sun's heat, combined with last night's lack of sleep and the comedown from the morning's combat, is beginning to make people drowsy.

I sit in the shade of a small tree, opposite the soldiers as they wait. Some smoke, others look shattered. All seems peaceful. Wrong. CRACKCRACKCRACK! Bark, leaves, and branches tumble onto me as the small tree is raked with gunfire. Not having any more substantial cover, I press myself into the ground and stab the record button on the camera as I do so, a habit that I have tried to cultivate over the last few days: start rolling as soon as the fighting starts. The Estonian soldiers, who are already in positions, their drowsy reverie instantly forgotten, do not return fire. There is no sign of the enemy. It was a hit and run. Of all the bullets that have passed in my general direction over the last few days, it is these ones that feel the most personal; I was the only one sitting by the tree, and therefore it was me being peered at through a rifle sight. Not a nice feeling.

Then, some awful news. Karli listens into his radio headset for a moment, and turns to me. 'That was a group of ten- to twelve-year-old boys,' he says. 'The Taliban gave them weapons and told them to attack us.' For a moment, everybody is speechless. Using kids to fight? One of the British soldiers hangs his head and spits a string of swear words. War is a questionable business at the best of times, but takes on an edge of sickening wrongness when children are involved.

3.00 p.m.—It has all been silent for a while now. The sun is slowly roasting us here in this compound, only blocked by the shade of the bullet-ridden tree, which nobody wants to take shelter under. Raigo informs us to prepare to pull out of the village, back to the scrapyard. I am confused—this doesn't make sense—why have we just risked our lives to take a village, just to pull out of it a few hours later? 'It's about pushing the enemy back,' Rob explains. 'If we give them something to think about here, then the Afghan police and army in Lashkar Gar—which is just to the south—will be safer. They will have fewer attacks against them, and more of a chance to provide security to the people there.' It makes sense, but is slightly depressing, nonetheless.

6.00 p.m.—We are all back at our mound in the scrapyard, trading war stories. Juri's new child was almost made fatherless; Taliban bullets missed him by less than a yard. Neil shot an enemy fighter that was attempting to sneak through the trees toward him. Everybody is relieved that they didn't have to make the decision to shoot the child fighters, who ran away before anyone could engage them. Nobody wants the death of a child on their conscience, whether they are enemy combatants or not. As the sun begins to set, sentries are posted and we go to bed. I continue my nightly habit of staring up at the moon, thanking God for watching over us today.

TUESDAY 10 MARCH

1.00 a.m.—Rob shakes me awake. 'Get up,' he whispers, 'we might be about to be attacked.' I am instantly awake. Intercepted radio messages from the Taliban are coming through to tell us they have us surrounded, that they are laying bombs and setting ambushes for us. I suddenly feel very exposed on this mound. The clear moon, earlier a source of peace and comfort, is now a treacherous light; an unwelcome silver lamp revealing our position to our enemies around us. I peer into the dark, twisted wreckage of the scrap heap. Do I see movement? Or are fatigue and darkness playing tricks on me? Every soldier holds their rifle ready, waiting patiently for something to happen. An hour, two hours pass. Silence. I can hear distant crickets, merrily chirping away. We spend the rest of the night in a state of readiness—any sleep had is fitful, and uneasy.

8.00 a.m.—BOOM! A distant, mushroom-shaped dark cloud blooms in the middle distance. We survived the night; no Taliban attack ever came. Now it seems that, having set up as many bombs as possible during the dark hours, they may have scored an 'own goal'. The Taliban often fall prey to their own devices, whether through incompetence, faulty technology or sheer bad luck.

But the reality is more bleak. About fifteen minutes after the explosion, we see a white minivan tearing through the scrapyard toward us. The Estonians ready their weapons. Is this a suicide bomber? It's coming at us very fast, swerving slightly erratically. There are several people inside— good news, as suicide bombers usually work alone. The soldiers hold their fire. The vehicle screeches to a halt, and an Afghan policeman jumps out, motioning frantically to us. Inside the vehicle are a family of locals. Blood is everywhere. Their bodies are mangled. Some are still alive. The policeman tells us the explosion we heard was result of this family driving over one of the bombs that the Taliban had set. There were eight people in their vehicle when it exploded. Some were killed immediately. Some are still dying.

The Estonian medics immediately set to work. Neil radios Camp Bastion, asking for a medevac. Among the family are two small boys, no more than eight years old. Their faces are bloody, and caked with dust. They stare blankly into space as the medics work on them. One has a large piece of shrapnel embedded in his stomach. I see Juri looking on in abject horror—I can imagine that he is superimposing his son's face onto these boys in his mind. Ergo is crouched beside one of the boys, grimacing. Everyone is quiet. The 'beep … beep …' from the Estonian ambulance's life support monitor cuts through the air. Neil confirms there are two helicopters on the way.

One of the men dies. The boy with the shrapnel is his stomach looks to be fading fast. There is a distant 'wakkawakkawakka' as we hear the helicopters approaching. The Taliban open fire on them as they approach. Hatred bubbles amongst the soldiers. How dare these people—if we can even call them that—shoot at a medical helicopter that is coming to try and save children that they blew up? Thankfully, as usual, their aim is wild, and the helicopters are able to land. The wounded are placed aboard, and flown off to Camp Bastion. We find out soon after that the shrapnel boy didn't make it.

11.00 a.m.—The operation is over and, in poignant silence, we prepare to head back to Lashkar Gar for a day's rest, before traveling down to Patrol Base Jaker. Looking at the soldiers in my vehicle, I can see that we are all thinking about that explosion, and those children. We are also thinking about the other bombs that the Taliban planted last night—are we going to make it back intact? Neil intently watches the video feed from the pilots above. Reports come through that the Taliban are preparing to attack us as we leave. I feel sick in my stomach. I can't believe I obsessively sought out combat for so long. The old military maxim offered by veterans to young, action-hungry soldiers comes into my mind: 'be careful what you wish for'. Regardless, we all make it to Lashkar Gar without incident. Mission complete.

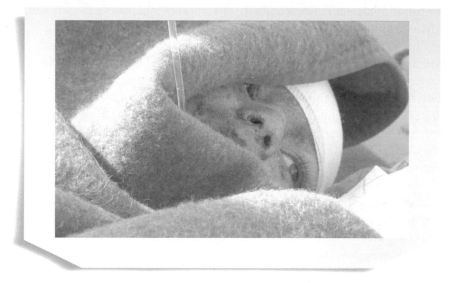

The Afghan boy who later died from his injuries.

7 Jaker

11 March 2009—26 March 2009

WEDNESDAY 11 MARCH

Spending the day resting in 'Lash Vegas'. I phone Mel immediately to let her know that I have managed to get some cracking combat footage—she is very happy for me, and asks me to send footage back so we can give it to the Estonian media. A British officer kindly lets me borrow his internet connection for the purpose. I feel like I am floating today—having survived my first real combat operation is an amazing feeling, and even mundane activities seem astonishing. I thank God repeatedly for getting me through it, and giving me the courage to do what I needed to do under fire.

8.00 p.m.—We have a rough screening of my footage for the Estonian soldiers tonight, before we head to Jaker. Soldiers cheer and whoop when they see themselves in action, people laugh and celebrate when they relive close calls, they fall silent when shots of the wounded civilians appear. It's an odd atmospere.

THURSDAY 12 MARCH

3.00 a.m.—I am getting used to these ridiculously early starts. I travel in Juri's vehicle today, sharing the back with a very excitable Estonian who proudly shows off the various small wood carvings he has created during his time here, and amicably talks my ear off every time I try to catch a bit of shuteye. I forgive him—everyone seems upbeat after the events of the last few days, and just being alive is a wonderful feeling.

11.00 a.m.—Finally arrive in Jaker, where I help unload the water and food supplies for the troops here. There is a British OMLT unit who, with their Afghan counterparts, are about to go on a patrol. After checking with Raigo—the Estonians aren't doing anything today—I ask if I can accompany them. The platoon commander agrees, and briefs me on the patrol ahead. We are heading three kilometres north of Jaker, and will be patrolling in an area which has seen heavy fighting in recent weeks. There is a large concentration of Taliban in this area, but the OMLT are not sure whether anything will happen this afternoon. One of the British soldiers, 'Dan', takes me aside and politely asks if it would be OK for me not to film him. He is hoping to try out for the SAS soon, and would therefore prefer that his face not appear in any footage. No problem.

1.00 p.m.—There are about thirty of us in total—an equal mix of Afghan and British soldiers. It takes two waves of vehicles to ferry us to the patrol departure point. The Afghans stand around in a gaggle, talking and laughing loudly. The British soldiers sit in the baking sun, making sure that there is no sign of the enemy. The green grass waves gently in the breeze. I feel extremely tired, and begin to regret coming on this patrol. It seems extremely peaceful—no Taliban radio communications at all—and I wish that I could be back at Jaker, resting with the Estonian soldiers there. After waiting about thirty minutes for the Afghan commander to turn up (Afghan officers have a bit of a reputation for being late and reluctant to partake in patrol duty) we finally head off.

The OMLT are slightly stricter than the Estonians: I am not given an option of where I go, and get put with the rear section of soldiers. We will be at the back of the patrol, coming forward only if there is a need for it. We wait as the Afghan soldiers and the rest of the OMLT in the front sections begin to head out. It's then our turn, and we shake out into a loose line to begin walking. With all the patrols I have been on by now, I have a fairly good formula for camera work: three close ups of boots walking, eight close ups of soldier's faces, six wide shots of the entire patrol walking the line, and so forth. It's not a hard and fast checklist, but it hasn't let me down yet.

Still no sign of the Taliban. It feels like a nice walk in the sun. Since the recent combat, simple things like this have taken on a whole new dimension of pleasure in my mind. My stomach rumbles, and I am looking forward to getting back to Jaker for some food and rest. I'll enjoy this peaceful walk, get the shots I need, and get back to base, job done.

We walk into an open field, sticking to the dirt track. The ground is heavily irrigated by the nearby Helmand River, and the mud is soft and slimy. The other two front sections are about two hundred meters off to the front and right, and a cool breeze wafts across my face. This is nice. CRACK CRACK CRACK! WHIZZ! WHIZZ! Panic. Out of nowhere, the Taliban have engaged us. 'Contact, wait out!' comes over the net. The other two sections are being engaged as well. We throw ourselves into an irrigation ditch next to the path where the long grass shields us from view. Bullets continue to crack, pop, and whizz around us. The platoon commander—who is with our section—shouts out to us. 'Guys, get back into the trees!'

We passed through a thin line of trees before we came out into the open field which, despite offering sparse cover, are infinitely more promising

Taliban bullets landing around us. Note that everybody is hugging the ground!

than grass. CRACK! CRACK! 'Go, now!' he yells. We begin to peel off—a standard military manoeuvre—toward the trees. There is an Afghan soldier running in front of me. I hate being exposed like this, completely in the open. CRACK! The Afghan soldier is running very slowly; I am snapping at his heels. Realise suddenly that I am maintaining formation behind him merely because I was always taught to do so in the Army. I am no longer a soldier, and I am not going to risk my life for the sake of a formation! I quickly overtake him, and throw myself gratefully into the trees. Once there I film the rest of the soldiers arrive, hoping that nobody will get shot on camera.

Dirt kicks up around us, bark splinters, leaves get hit and fall lazily onto us. So this is what it is like to be properly suppressed, I think to myself. We are lying flat on the ground. An Afghan soldier several meters away from me has thrown away his weapon, and is lying like a starfish, not even wanting to lift his head. A bullet hits a patch of earth to my right and sends up a puff of dust. Sinister cracks and snaps have become our world. It is absolutely terrifying. A British soldier to my left swears loudly as a bullet whizzes just about his head. Despite the situation, we laugh. It's unreal. BOOM! An RPG is fired, but thankfully misses. The soldiers with me are unable to engage the Taliban, because they are unsure where the other sections are and don't want to risk killing their friends. CRACK! HISS! WHIZZ! This is not fun. A message comes over the radio, two words that nobody in any army ever wants to hear. Man down.

Somebody—we aren't sure who—in one of the lead sections has been hit. He is in a critical condition, and will die if he is not rescued. We are the rear section. The reserve section. The casualty evacuation section. We have to move. The platoon commander tells us that we have to go. There are blank looks of fear from both Afghan and British soldiers. We have just been hugging the ground, praying for our lives, and now we have to get up and run through the bullet-infested air. I am shaking, but I resolve not to be the one who refuses to move. Lord, I pray in my head, I ask that you watch over me now, and if I am to die, please can it be as painless as possible. 'Go!' It's time to get up. My arms and legs scream at me as I force them to make me stand. We begin to run. CRACK!

We jump into a stream beside a tall bank, which the platoon

commander plans to use it as cover as we try to get to the casualty. The beloved, sweet, thick bank runs out far sooner than I had hoped, and before long we are pounding through an open, boggy field, which greedily sucks at my boots as I try to run. I am so, so glad for the endless laps of the base in Kabul with my heavy bag on—I think that I'd be having a heart attack about now otherwise. CRACK CRACK! That was close. I sink to the ground for a second to compose my thoughts. This is insane. No time to dwell on it. Dan is close behind me. I clamber to my feet and keep going. Right foot, left foot. Squelch squelch squelch. I hear the distant sound of an Apache arriving. I want to kiss it; our deadly, beautiful guardian angel.

We get to a compound, the last bit of cover before the open field where the casualty lies. Inside the compound a dog, presumably driven mad by the firefight, is throwing itself around, barking madly, and snapping at the soldiers who try to gain access. 'Shoot it!' someone says. An Afghan soldier raises his rifle and snaps a shot off at the dog, hitting it in the stomach. The miserable animal whines and begins to shake, sinking to the ground. It fixes us with a stare. 'Why are you doing this to me?' it seems to say. 'I am just protecting my home.'

'Don't just leave him like that!' A British soldier swears at the Afghan. The Afghan nods, aims his rifle for a second time, and shoots the dog in the head. We have no time to reflect on this. There is a man that needs our help. Before we get out into the open, the platoon commander turns to assess us. 'Right, who's going to carry the stretcher?' There isn't a flurry of volunteers. I look around. Some of the soldiers here are very young. Their eyes are wide open. They are terrified. The interpreter, an Afghan soldier, and Dan volunteer. 'Sir,' I find myself saying, 'I used to be in the Paras—we had to do stretcher races all the time, I'll do it too.' He nods.

We run out into the open. CRACK CRACK! The fact that the Taliban have not immediately run away from an Apache shows that there must be a fairly sizeable group of them. I am absolutely terrified. I pray as I run, while pushing the Afghan soldier who is stumbling in front of me, his strength flagging. In my mind, God's words to Joshua—the man I was named for—in the Bible suddenly come to me:

Exhausted and terrified, we approach the orange smoke that marks where the casualty is.

'Have I not commanded you? Be strong and courageous. Do not be afraid; do not be discouraged, for the Lord your God will be with you wherever you go.' (Joshua 1:9)

I know that God has ordained that I am here, in this moment, running toward the casualty with the other soldiers. I know that he is completely and utterly in control of this situation. Despite my fear, I feel peace wash over me; I know that he is with me. I repeat his words to Joshua over and over as I run through the bog and the grass.

An orange smoke grenade bursts about fifty meters away, marking the location of the casualty. We are heaving with exhaustion, numb-legged, and the last few steps drag on and on. What we arrive at is not a pleasant sight. I immediately turn my camera off—now is not the time to gather footage. He has been shot in the face. The bullet has sliced through jaw and cheek, and emerged on the other side. His tongue, wet with dark blood, is hanging out, touching his ear. I never realized that tongues could be that long. His face has a pale green tinge to it. The medic, a young blonde Navy girl called Kate, frantically works on him, inserting a breathing tube into his nose. His mouth is too clogged with blood and ragged flesh for him to breathe unaided. We move him to the stretcher, where Kate will have to tend to him as we run. I pick up her rifle. It's the first time I have touched a British rifle since 2007, but muscle memory comes back to me instantly. I remove the magazine, and make the weapon safe. One of the soldiers looks at me curiously; it is probably odd to see a cameraman proficiently clearing a loaded weapon. I sling the rifle behind my back—I have no intention of using it, just carrying it so nobody else is encumbered with it—and hook my camera around my neck.

We pick up the stretcher: the wounded man is heavy with bulky gear. We sink deeper into the mud. 'Go! Go! Go!' the commander shouts, and we pound forward as fast as we can. I have never known physical exertion like it—none of the brutal Para selection tests even come close to this level of agony. Hands burn, legs shake, breath is ragged. The soldiers shout at each other to keep going. They shout to the injured man—who I find out is called Jon—to hang on, telling him he will be OK. I wonder if they actually believe what they are saying. To me, it looks like he is going to die. We reach the bank of a deep stream. The slippery mud works against us, and we almost fall in, taking Jon with us. I decide to jump in the water to help stabilize the stretcher from below. We run, and we run, and we run. Angry, panicked voices berate any who don't put every ounce of effort into getting Jon out of there. A British medical Chinook is on its way, and we don't want to keep it waiting with the Taliban around.

After what seems like three hours of running—although it's probably only about twenty minutes or so—we finally reach the makeshift HLS, that other soldiers have secured. The 'whump-whump-whump' of the Chinook descends to surround us. 'Cover the casualty!' someone screams, as the heat, grass, and dust kicked up by the Chinook thrash at our faces. We throw ourselves over and around Jon, protecting his open wounds from the cloying dust. Once it has settled, we pick him up and run him over to the Chinook. The medics take him, and within an instant, he is gone.

Silence. Birds sing. Crickets chirp. I sink to the floor and rub the sweat from my face. Soldiers begin to check that everyone is OK. We drink water, lots of water. I wring the wet filth of the stream from my socks, and feel at a complete loss for what to say. I have never experienced anything remotely like this afternoon in my life. Everybody is congratulating Kate: she ran across an open field, under fire, to save Jon with no regard whatsoever for her safety. Several soldiers thank me for helping when, as a media guy, I could have just sat there and not got involved. I thank God, for giving me the strength to volunteer myself.

6.00 p.m.—Finally arrive in Jaker after a long, silent march back, under the watchful eye of two circling Apaches. Pete walks up to me as I remove my sweaty body armour and helmet. He has a steaming plate of ration pack macaroni cheese. 'Here you go, mate,' he says, 'you deserve it.' Nothing has ever tasted nicer.

We receive reports from Bastion that Jon is going to live. I lie in the dust on my camp bed and watch the moon. Tears fill my eyes. 'Thank you, Lord.'

FRIDAY 13 MARCH

The Estonians head out on a two-day operation in Nawa, the area around PB Jaker. I accompany them—this will probably be the last assignment with them before we head back to Lashkar Gar in a few days. I will go onto Kabul from there. After yesterday's events, my desire for action and excitement is at its all-time lowest ebb. I would be perfectly happy if we spend two days blundering around in the Green Zone doing nothing. It is a long, hot day, and I am with Juri's platoon again, with Neil tagging along to provide any aerial support that we might need. Several hours into the patrol, we stop an old man who has a small tattoo of a crescent moon on his hand. The interpreter tells us it is likely this man is involved with the Taliban in some way—the tattoo is a fairly common mark among their fighters.

6.00 p.m.—It's been a mercifully quiet day so far. The Taliban pop up on the airwaves now and then, but their talk smacks of the usual bravado, without much actual willingness to do anything. As the sun begins to set, however, they begin to make serious plans to launch an attack on the compound we are staying in. The aircraft above us, a pair of French F16s, cannot see anything, and so Neil—partly to scare the Taliban, and partly for my benefit—ask them to do a 'show of force'. They duly oblige, screaming low over our heads and launching flares. It's very loud, awe-inspiring, and—I imagine, if I was a Taliban—terrifying. We don't hear a peep out of them for the rest of the day.

11.00 p.m.—Neil tells us that there is going to be a big US Special Forces raid further up north tonight, in the area where Jon was shot yesterday. It's going to be a very large operation, and our role is to stay in the compound; all eyes are going to be on them.

I fall asleep, waking only once during the night to the sound of distant aircraft and muffled bangs.

SATURDAY 14 MARCH

Neil tells me that in the raid last night, eight Taliban were killed, and fifty taken prisoner. Astounding numbers—it's usually the other way round. They must have been so overwhelmed, so quickly, that they had no time to mount an effective resistance. Taliban activity in this area will have taken a serious hit. We finish the operation, and head back to Jaker. I am relieved to get there.

SUNDAY 15 MARCH

We are told that we aren't to leave the base today. It's Helmand polio vaccination day, run by a charity, and it would be disastrous to have a running gunfight while the already nervous locals were being immunized. I spend the day in the sun, wearing a pair of the nigh-on indecent, flesh-coloured, Danish underwear and reading a book. It's nice to relax after the last few days. The Estonian soldiers—in similar states of undress—also lounge around, playing cards, attempting to cook, and watching DVDs.

CRACK! CRACK! Apparently the Taliban didn't get the memo about no gunfights. Once again, in flagrant disregard of any common battlefield courtesy, they attack. Bullets spatter against the walls of Jaker. I throw on my helmet, body armour, and boots and start to record the firefight. I fervently hope that nobody takes a photo of me in this state: it's visually offensive. I look like a sorry sight, running round with my underwear, skinny white legs, and combat gear. The Estonians, similarly clad in shorts, helmets, and armour, return fire and repel the Taliban assault. Nobody is injured. We laugh about it afterwards.

8.00 p.m.—Lying next to a vehicle, falling asleep. A distant popping 'thud'. That sounds a lot like a rocke- WHEEEEEEEEEW! The whistle of incoming artillery is terrifying. For a few seconds of abject terror, I feel utterly alone. There is a shell above me tearing earthward, and there is every chance it will come down on top of me. I cannot do anything about it, except press my face into the dirt and say a split second prayer. BOOOOM! The rocket lands in the base. There is a moment of silence, and then some shouting. Somebody has been hit. An Afghan soldier suffered an almost direct hit, his body almost totally destroyed in an instant. Another is seriously wounded. A Chinook is called to pick them up. There are three rocket attacks in total throughout the night, each one ushering in a paralyzing fear that lasts until a nearby explosion tells me that I have survived. These were just three shells. I can see why people in previous wars—under constant bombardment—lost their minds.

MONDAY 16 MARCH

Drive back to Lashkar Gar today in Raigo's vehicle. We are greeted by rear troops that insist that we be deloused before being allowed to walk around base. An odd end to a surreal couple of weeks. I call Mel and Will to tell them about my time in Jaker, since there was very little mobile signal in Nawa. Will asks me how I am feeling, and we talk about the various experiences I have been through. There isn't even a hint of jealousy in his voice—I realize that we are long past that, and that he has become a real friend. I am really looking forward to seeing him and Mel soon. I say goodbye to the Estonians, Rob, Pete, and Neil. Once again, I am astonished by what the bond of shared combat does to people—I will be genuinely sad to leave them, and can't stomach the idea of not being with them in forthcoming operations. Thankfully, they are all finishing their deployment in a few weeks, so I am hoping they all make it through. I return to Bastion.

TUESDAY 17 MARCH

I have a flight to Kabul tonight, and pass the time hanging around the Estonian NSE in Bastion. Maarte, the logistics officer, comes up to me, asking how it was. I immediately begin to gush about what an amazing experience it was, and how great the combat footage turned out to be. A flicker of disappointment crosses his face. I realize, with great shame, that I have broken my promise to him about not just focussing on the frontline troops. I haven't filmed anything about the logistical side of things at all, and it's too late now to correct the balance.

10.00 p.m.—Arrive back in Kabul. The cool night air is a pleasant contrast to the heat of Helmand. Mel and Will are waiting for me as I walk off the rear ramp of the Hercules. We rarely actually turn up to greet each other at the terminal, seeing that our accommodation is about five hundred meters away, but tonight they want to welcome me back and support me. Mel has saved me some food—which is great, as I am starving. I talk to them about the trip. It's really good to be back with my family. I lie in bed that night and thank God for all he has done over the past few weeks, for being with me, and keeping me safe. I chuckle to myself as I think about the irony of striving to get into action over the past year, yearning for some sort of recognition and glory, and then putting it all aside and resolving to trust in God, who took care of the situation far better than I could have ever imagined.

I begin to notice that there is a difference between 'vending machine faith' and real faith. Vending machine faith is only going to God when you want something for yourself, fervently hoping that he gives you what you ask for, and then becoming uninterested in him the moment you get it, or the instant your hopes fall through. Real faith is giving it all to him, deciding to trust him regardless of what happens, making him your number one goal, your number one satisfaction, and accepting whatever comes.

THURSDAY 19 MARCH

David's replacement arrives today. Her name is Ruth. It's going to be weird having a new face in our team, but we resolve to make her feel as welcome as possible. Mel and I greet her as she arrives. She is eager to get stuck in.

1.00 p.m.—I take Ruth to HQ ISAF to try and secure her ID. After my time in Helmand, I am finding it hard to deal with the bureaucracy and the attitude of the soldiers here who never leave the base. My attitude is not right, and I catch myself slipping into expletive-ridden rants to the newly arrived Ruth. I really don't want to fall back into who I was before.

WEDNESDAY 25 MARCH

Working like a madman to try and get these Estonian stories finished by the time I go on leave tomorrow. I am cutting a small series called 'Taking the Fight to the Taliban'. Estonian media are snapping it up—they are showing the footage on their TV stations, talking about it in their newspapers, and it's all over their social media. It's genuinely great to see the bravery and good work of their few soldiers feature like this; it's not often that they get much media coverage.

THURSDAY 26 MARCH

Checking in for the flight back to Denmark. I signed a contract renewal with Thomas this week; I will be here for one more year at least. I stare out of the plane's window as clouds roll languidly past—I wonder what the next twelve months will hold. Whatever it is, I just want to make sure that I face it with God.

8 Heat

12 April 2009—31 May 2009

SUNDAY 12 APRIL

My first Sunday back in the UK. I spent last weekend in Croatia, visiting some friends. During previous periods of leave, I would attend church out of habit, maintaining the illusion that 'all is well' with me, despite not caring too much at all. This time, it all feels different. I want to be here.

TUESDAY 21 APRIL

Meet up with Dan in London. He is working for a major news channel now. It isn't the same in Afghanistan without him, but it's good to see that he is doing well for himself. He listens eagerly as I tell him about the Estonian mission, and Patrol Base Jaker—I am finally able to understand the sights, smells, and feelings of the kind of real combat experience he faced last summer. We eventually part company, and I wish him all the best with his new job.

WEDNESDAY 29 APRIL

Sitting on a train to Heathrow airport. Sun pours into the windows. It's going to be much hotter in Afghanistan than here. Here we go again.

FRIDAY 1 MAY

Back in Kabul. My first trip during this long summer stint is going to be with the Australians down south in Uruzgan, the province north of

Helmand. I depart on Monday morning. Before I go, however, there is the small matter of the annual DANCON race which I wish to address. DANCON, or 'Danish Contingent', puts on a twenty-two kilometre race, in whichever base they have soldiers, during May every year. Participants are required to run it with a helmet and body armour on their person—in the Afghan heat, this is no mean feat. Being fitter than I have for quite some time, I am looking forward to taking part in this. The only problem is that since the combat in March, I have been getting sharp spikes of pain in my hip when I run.

6.00 p.m.—Hip not good. I went for a small run, and had to stop due to the pain. It does not bode well for the race tomorrow. As I lie down, I pray. 'Lord, I know that you are in control of all things—even my hip. You know that I'd like to take part in the race tomorrow, please can you heal me.' Despite the changes in my life, I realise that I am still pretty 'me centred', a hallmark of spiritual immaturity.

SATURDAY 2 MAY

5.00 a.m.—Wake up, race time. We have to start early because of the sun—nobody wants to be running by midday. I stretch and flex my legs. No hip pain. Jog on the spot. Nothing. Make my way down to start point. The race will consist of one massive lap around Kabul airbase, which—with some detours and double-backs thrown in—makes up the required twenty-two kilometres.

On the start line are bleary-eyed soldiers from the variety of national contingents that make up our base. The Danish NSE commander, Marcus—Bo left a while ago—starts the race. I take off at a brisk jog. No pain whatsoever.

8.00 a.m.—Reach the end in a panting, sweaty heap. I finish second, which was good—a mysterious Belgian special forces soldier overtook me two-thirds of the way through the race, grinning and patting me on the shoulder as he ran past. Although I am aching all over, I cannot believe that I didn't have any hip pain, despite suffering from it for over a month. An interesting thought—why am I surprised that God answered my prayer? Does that mean that when I prayed for healing, I didn't actually think that he would answer me? Mulling this over, I pass out in my bed.

MONDAY 4 MAY

Fly down to Uruzgan. I am perfectly happy for this to be a quiet trip; there are rumblings at HQ about several large Helmand operations this summer which I may well end up in, so the prospect of a peaceful jaunt with the Australians seems good to me.

THURSDAY 7 MAY

On a long Green Zone patrol with Australian soldiers today—we slog our way through rivers, fields, and small forests. Earlier Jurassic Park comparisons aside, the scenery really does give us the feel of a band of adventurers marooned in the Mesozoic. Everything bursts with floral vibrancy; deep, green and alien. Hay fever flares up as weird and wonderful pollen graces the air about me.

FRIDAY 8 MAY

Sitting in an Afghan police outpost on the verges of the green zone. Afghan army and Australian soldiers are also here. The Australians are a good bunch. While their behaviour smacks endearingly of all the Aussie stereotypes that I have heard of, there is so much more to them than Antipodean cliché. We conduct daily patrols out of their base—always with Afghan soldiers or policeman in tow, in accordance with ISAF policy this year—into the Green Zone. There is little Taliban activity. The soldiers here have only been in a couple of firefights during their entire six-month tour.

3.00 p.m.—BANG! I nearly jump out of my skin as a gunshot goes off right behind me. It's an Afghan soldier who was being rather careless with the handling of his weapon. The bullet flies harmlessly off into the air. The world-weary Aussies berate him, but judging by the looks on their faces, it seems this is a fairly regular occurrence.

WEDNESDAY 13 MAY

Fly back to Kabul today. The Danish soldiers have asked if our team could give them one of our rooms back. I suspect they have become tired of seeing the chaos of my room, which goes against every regimented military bone in their bodies, and quite reasonably they commandeer it. I am to move next door with Will. Neither of us bemoans the loss of privacy too much, since we tend to spend a most of our free time together anyway. Finding the lamest-sounding movies we can, we subject ourselves to repeated marathons of charmingly terrible cinema.

SATURDAY 16 MAY

I see a small A4 poster—rather dog-eared—on the sun-bleached notice board beside our dining facility, and make out the words 'Worship Service—Come to Chapel on Sundays, 7.00 pm!' I didn't even realize there was a chapel on this base—not surprising, given that over the past year I had little interest in finding one—and it turns out I have been walking past it for the past twelve months on my way to eat. It's a small, ramshackle building made out of planks. I resolve to check it out tomorrow.

SUNDAY 17 MAY

7.00 p.m.—Go to chapel. It's nicer than it looked from outside. There are small wooden benches, and an ornate table in the middle. A man named Wes—an American contractor working here—takes the service. He used to be a preacher in the past and, due to a lack of chaplains at our base, he has taken it on himself to keep the chapel running smoothly. Not many attend, twelve tonight, but it's really nice to be here. I am the only non-American to attend.

MONDAY 25 MAY

Flying down to Helmand today, on my first visit there since the frenetic combat operations of March. I am heading to the northern part of Helmand, to a town called Musa Qaleh, where British forces will be launching an operation. There has been hard fighting over possession of this town in recent years. In the summer of 2006, a few soldiers from the Para battle group had to hold it against repeated Taliban attacks. After a few months, a deal was brokered with local elders to ensure that both ISAF troops and Taliban would leave the town. There was much opposition to this move, with many people declaring it 'a British retreat', and sure enough after a few months the Taliban re-entered Musa Qala, and took control, much to the muted chorus of 'I told you so' from many British and American officers. The town was retaken by force in 2007, and held ever since by British and Afghan soldiers.

3.00 p.m.—Board the Chinook to Musa Qala. Mail, supplies, and bags are piled around us. If this helicopter gets shot down, I imagine that it will be a flying tin of liver pate that will finish me off. It's a fairly long flight by Helmand travel standards, but we reach the town centre base in one piece. A sunburnt female officer meets me: she is the unit press officer for the guys about to conduct the operation. I am taken on a brief tour of the base. As per every site in Helmand, it is a fairly grim affair—hot, dusty, and sweaty, with very few amenities. In the centre of the camp is a broken down building—much like the one at PB Jaker—where some of the more privileged ranks get to sleep. I am given a dark concrete room at the bottom, but as I walk into it, I suddenly feel like a pie that is being placed into an oven—it is very, very hot in here. I decide to keep the flies and mosquitoes company by sleeping outside.

7.00 p.m.—Two other journalists arrive, much to my immediate worry. My experience with other journalists during my brief stint with the US Marines last summer was not pleasant, and I have no desire to be roped into a similar situation again.

Thankfully, what happens next serves to demonstrate just why forming judgement on a preconceived idea is completely wrong. The two guys, one a writer, and the other a photographer, are absolutely brilliant company. They work for a major British tabloid newspaper, but carry none of the attitude that I have observed in other such people. We all bed down under the stars, flies and other insects repeatedly tormenting us. It is a hot and sleepless night.

TUESDAY 26 MAY

Spend the day killing time in the base. It's not a pleasant affair, and so I decide to try and distract myself by getting stuck into a book that endeavours to answer some of the most difficult questions about Christianity. The central question is arguably the most problematic in theology—'why does God allow evil and suffering to exist?' Needless to say, that question has begun to play more and more on my mind this year, as due consequence of my proximity to the nastier side of life out here in a war zone. The suffering chapter is several hundred pages in, and I refrain from skipping ahead.

WEDNESDAY 27 MAY

11.00 p.m.—It's probably unwise to be up so late. It has been a very restless couple of days with the ever-present heat making sleep extremely fitful, and I am heading out to the forward bases tomorrow, but I am desperate to catch the European Champions League football final tonight. Manchester United—playing for their second final in a row—are playing against Barcelona. If they win, they will be the first team in history to retain the cup. Needless to say, they are soundly beaten, and I find myself wishing that I had gone to bed earlier.

THURSDAY 28 MAY

7.00 a.m.—I travel in a convoy of heavily armoured vehicles to FOB Minden, the base that will serve as launch pad for the operation due to kick off tomorrow. British troops are packed into the dusty compounds, cleaning their weapons, playing cards, and calling loved ones back home. I find that I am getting the pre-operation nervousness that I had last time, except that the excitement—which had made the former bearable—is no longer present. I know what combat is like now. It is exciting. It is terrifying. It is deadly.

I make myself busy by seeking out people to interview, one of whom is the youngest British soldier currently serving in Helmand. He has very recently turned eighteen, and as I talk to him I think back to what I was doing on my eighteenth birthday. I was nowhere near flying bullets and rocket attacks, that's for sure.

2.00 p.m.—The company commander of the soldiers I am with—the Royal Welsh—calls us round a large rectangular area marked out in the sand. Somebody has painstakingly turned it into a map of the mission's objective using rocks, cups, bits of metal, and any other detritus to form a map that would do the Ordnance Survey proud. It's an impressive effort. The operation, named 'Mar Lewe', aims to clear a nearby village, Yatimchay, of enemy fighters. Listening to the brief being given, I am reminded of my first village clearance operation with the Estonians. The only difference here, it seems, is that the soldiers will be holding the territory and going on to build a small base, so as not to hand the hard-won ground back to the Taliban the moment troops pull out of the village.

I will be accompanying some of the soldiers as they deploy into the village and begin to clear compounds. Nervous.

8.00 p.m.—Lie in the dust, reading my camouflage Bible before I go to sleep. Its formerly white pages are adopting a rather brownish hue. It is fast becoming a veteran. I read about some of my heroes in the Old Testament—David and Joshua specifically, guys who fought in numerous battles. I wonder how they felt the night before a battle. Did they get nervous? Their declarations of trust in God, the full extent of which I found lost on me when I was safely back home in the UK, mean so much more on the eve of potential combat. Lord, teach me to have the same faith in you as these men did.

FRIDAY 29 MAY

3.00 a.m.—I am prodded awake. There are muted red torches gyrating around me, and the soldiers begin to pack away their kit, ready for mission launch. As with various other nocturnal adventures I have been on, it is important for everybody to get into position before the sky is light. I climb into the back of a British Warrior armoured vehicle—it is dark, hot, and cramped. There are six of us crammed into the back like tragic sardines, sweating and staring at each other with gummy eyes in the murky red glow.

After an excruciating wait, the armoured brute growls itself to life, and we lurch out into the desert. There are no windows in this vehicle, and therefore any situational awareness extends purely to the information that is being passed through to the sergeant, Matt, sitting beside me.

5.00 a.m.—A loud 'BOOOOM!' Hard to tell how far away it is. Was it an IED? Has one of the British vehicles been hit? Matt chatters into his headset for a moment, and turns to the rest of the soldiers in the vehicle. 'We just dropped a five hundred pound bomb on the Taliban leader's compound—they think that they got him.' Decapitating the leader of the insurgents in this area will surely have an effect on the outcome of this battle. Despite the fact that somebody has just died, the soldiers beside me cannot help but feel cheered by the news. Their day has just become potentially less hazardous.

6.00 a.m.—Our Warrior stops—we have reached our initial objective. It's time for the soldiers to start clearing the compounds. Here we go. 'Go! Go! Go!' Matt screams, as we stumble out into the disorientating sunlight, blinking as our eyes try to adjust from the pitch black of the Warrior to the harsh light of the Afghan sun. The compound is right next to us. A young Welsh soldier throws a ladder against the wall. 'Geddupthere! Geddupthere! Geddupthere!' Matt bellows as the poor chap clambers up. It has been confirmed that there are no civilians in this compound, and therefore the soldiers are clear to 'go in red'—i.e. with maximum firepower. The soldier atop the ladder begins to fire at buildings in the compound. Meanwhile, the Warrior barrels into one of the thick mud walls, creating a new entry for Matt and his men; conventional doors are likely to be booby-trapped.

The soldiers begin to clear the various buildings and outhouses of the compound in a cacophony of violence. 'BANG BANG BANG! BOOOM!' Grenades are tossed in each room. Adrenaline surges. A soldier with wide eyes turns each corner with a shotgun in his hand, expecting death at every turn. Matt is shouting. I film everything that I can.

The outhouses are clear—only the main house to go now. A soldier crouches and pours fire into the windows with his machine gun as one of his colleagues edges closer with a grenade. The idea is to pin the enemy down with fire, throw in a grenade, then finish them off by barrelling into the room with all guns blazing. The soldier with the grenade reaches the house, and I zoom in to get a good angle on him as he pulls the pin and prepares to chuck it through the window. 'GRENADE!' he bellows, and my breath jams in my throat as I notice several metal bars across the window. I hope his grenade misses them. It doesn't. In horrific slow-motion, the tight green ball of high explosives SPANGs off the bar and arcs toward us, landing in the middle of the soldiers. A moment of pure, terrifying silence as we try to process what has happened. 'GRENAAAAAADE!!' A dozen voices shout in unison as we dash for cover. Matt grabs me and we dive behind a corner. As we jump, I cannot help but think of those atrocious action films where the hero has to leap in slow-motion from an explosion behind him. I have become an awful parody of tha- BOOOOOOOOM! The grenade explodes, loudly, violently—for a moment, I pity anybody, friend or foe, that has ever been on the receiving end of one. Dust. Smoke. I wait for the call of 'man down!' There's no way that nobody was hurt in that. Coughs as people pick themselves up. 'Is everybody all right?' Matt yells. Muted grunts of affirmation. Nobody has even been scratched. I cannot believe it. I thank God repeatedly in my head. That would have been an awful way to go.

The compound is finally cleared. Matt finds two IEDs that were left for us by the Taliban. It is becoming fast apparent that they knew exactly when and where we were going to attack.

1.002 p.m.—We slog through Yatimchay, and meet up with other soldiers who have been clearing the compounds. There has been sporadic Taliban resistance, but nothing truly formidable. It seems that most of them withdrew before we arrived, and the early loss of their leader seems to have shattered any remaining resistance. 'WHEEEEEEEW! BOOOM!' A rocket screams over our heads and detonates nearby. We throw ourselves to the dusty floor. Despite the danger, everyone moves rather sluggishly— the sun is blazing down on us—and everybody is feeling exhausted. My helmet is too hot to touch. The Taliban fire another rocket at us: a parting shot.

We are moving very slowly. Soldiers at the front of our long column scan every step with metal detectors, hoping to find any bombs before they detonate. It is a thankless, enormously brave job. More often than not, it's the point men like these lose limbs and lives. One of the soldiers searching for bombs has 'PSALM 23' scrawled on the rim of his helmet. I am very moved—rarely will somebody walk through such an immediate, perilous 'valley of the shadow of death' as this young man. I hope he makes it.

6.00 p.m.—We set up for the next few days in another nameless compound. Everybody peels off sweaty body armour and gratefully slumps in the shade. I see the other journalists, who were attached to another unit. We compare notes—they were able to get a photo of the bomb dropping on the Taliban leader's compound, and I was able to get combat footage of the soldiers clearing buildings. We agree to share the material.

SATURDAY 30 MAY

3.00 p.m.—On patrol in Yatimchay. The British soldiers find an abandoned Taliban bomb factory. Evidence is gathered, and equipment is confiscated. Taliban bomb-making in this area—it is imagined—will take a serious hit from this find. Get good footage.

SUNDAY 31 MAY

Two British soldiers—part of another unit also participating in Op Mar

Lewe—are killed today when their vehicle hits a mine. We hear the distant explosion to the north of our position. The soldiers' zap numbers are passed over the radio (a zap number is a unique series of letters and numbers that make up an easy way of identifying somebody here. It consists of the first two letters of their surname, and the last four digits of their army number. For example, I was FO3699). Full names are not revealed at this stage, and every soldier who hears the casualty report over the radio begins to frantically work out if the zap numbers of the deceased belong to any of their friends. It is a desperate business, and what's even more tragic is that on the other side of the world, in the UK, two families are probably going about their Sundays normally, trying to relax, and perhaps occasionally sparing a thought for their loved ones who are over here. Little do they know that within a matter of hours, two smartly dressed soldiers will arrive at their doors, bringing them news that will shatter their worlds. Heartbreaking.

With the operation drawing to a close, and needing to pass some time before the helicopter arrives, I begin to read the 'Why does God allow evil and suffering?' chapter of my book. It feels more relevant than ever in light of the day's tragic news. It is a question that I have heard asked many times, and deep down within me, I have never known the answer. In brief, this is the argument presented:

Firstly, saying that 'evil and suffering prove that a loving God cannot exist' does not work. If we remove God from the equation, we are suddenly faced with a big problem—in a world of relative ideals and morals, who decides what is absolutely right? What makes us right, and the Taliban wrong? Unless there is a higher standard of what is good and what is evil, then morality becomes a very grey area. If we remove God, what is wrong with the natural order of violence, rape, theft, and deceit between human beings? We see examples of this in the animal world every day, and yet nobody deems it to be 'evil'. If we remove God, and are just animals, who is to say what Hitler did was wrong? After all, wasn't he just trying to create a 'super race' of humans: something that, from a perspective of natural struggle, could only be beneficial to the species? Martin Luther King said that the only way we can know if a human law or act is just is if there is a divine, higher law to compare it with.

The next part of the argument follows: 'if there is a God, why does evil also exist?' The writer then examines the beginning of evil. God created the world as perfect, but He also gave men and women free choice. It was their choice to reject God that caused the beginning of evil in the world. So why did God let them do that, if he is all-powerful? If he had created mindless automatons, programmed to love him, that wouldn't be very fulfilling. I can tell my mobile phone to come up with a reminder saying 'I love you' everyday, but that wouldn't mean it loves me. True love comes from somebody with free will choosing to love you. God loves us so much that he is willing to allow evil and suffering to exist—for the time being—so that human beings have the free choice to love him or not.

The writer then examines why evil and suffering are allowed to persist in the world. Why doesn't God just click his fingers and remove evil, pain, and suffering from the world? Well if he did do that, wouldn't everything be destroyed? After all, as human beings, we are not perfect people—we all commit evil acts. Just because evil and suffering are allowed to persist now, it doesn't mean that it will be like this indefinitely. Judgement delayed does not mean judgement denied. An example is then given: most people would say that there is a greater difference between human beings and God than there is between human beings and a bear. Well, say a bear is caught in a trap which is cutting into its leg, causing great pain. A friendly ranger comes along, eager to help the bear. In order to help the bear, however, he needs to momentarily tighten the trap in order to release it. The bear, feeling the increase of pain, does not understand that the ranger is working for his benefit, and lashes out angrily because he doesn't understand. In the same way suffering can be for our good, but often we don't understand it at the time. In fact, if you take the worst thing to ever happen on the planet you will see the point. The worst thing to ever happen on earth, by definition, is the murder of God.

And it's this that reveals God's attitude towards pain and suffering. The fact that Jesus—fully God, fully man—was murdered brutally on the cross tells us many things about the problem of pain and suffering. It tells us that God doesn't just fold his arms and watch impotently as the world suffers—he comes down and gets right in the middle of it, suffering with us. Jesus faced far greater pain and suffering during his time on earth than we could ever feel—the divine wrath of God poured out on him as he hung on the cross, and his subsequent three days in the grave were agony beyond compare. Even Jesus, during his suffering, cried out the question that we all experience during times of pain and suffering—'Why?'

Whatever else the cross shows, it demonstrates that God is not immune to suffering or pain; that he experiences it with us, and that he was willing to go through it, taking the punishment for all the evil that we have done on himself.

During times of pain and suffering, the primary thing that people need is not the answer to the question 'why?' but someone to be there with them, to help them in their pain. Jesus who, like us, has suffered, promises that he will never leave or forsake us if we turn to him.

I finish reading as the daylight begins to wane. It's one of the best answers I have ever heard to the problem of pain, evil, and suffering. Even such smooth logic as this, however, would do little to assuage the grief that the families of the two dead soldiers are about to face.

6.00 p.m.—The helicopter finally arrives. As I queue to board, the RAF crew motion to my T-shirt and shake their heads. It seems that a new health and safety rule has come into effect—long sleeves must be worn on all British helicopter flights. I begin to feverishly dig through my bag. Unpacking it hurriedly in the powerful rotor-wash of the Chinook is not a pleasant experience, and my fluster is compounded by the added pressure that any delay that keeps the chopper on the ground could be potentially dangerous. With great relief I find a crusty shirt right at the bottom, pull it on over my body armour—feeling more ridiculous than I have in a while—and proceed to board the helicopter. During the flight, one of the RAF guys gives me a thumbs-up by way of apology. He was just following rules. Lesson learnt—I'll wear a shirt in future.

9 Historic

15 June 2009—20 July 2009

MONDAY 15 JUNE

At HQ in Kabul. General McKiernan, the ISAF commander for the last year, was sacked a few weeks ago. It has been making headlines around the world; the last time a US general was sacked during operations was in the middle of the Second World War. Today, his successor is assuming the reins of command.

I set up the tripod and prepare to film. Assignments like this are usually the 'turd' stories we all dread. Regardless, I drew the short straw and must cover the event. The new commander, General Stanley McChrystal—a tall, gaunt man—takes to the podium and begins to address his new troops, the various diplomats who have gathered, and members of the world's press. He announces that there is going to be a significant change in the numbers of US troops present in Afghanistan (something that we have seen coming for a while now) and that this will be a decisive year for the war here. I have heard rhetoric like this before—indeed most people tend to disregard talk like this—but in this case, I stop and listen. McChrystal exudes something that I have never seen in a general before. There are several legends floating around the camp about him: he only eats one meal per day, he only sleeps four hours per night, he runs seven kilometres every morning, he listens to military training manuals and doctrine on his iPod. He was in command of Special Operations in Iraq during the decisive year of 2007, where his troops relentlessly demolished the Al-Qaeda network piece by piece. Judging by the looks of the various US military personnel present, he commands their respect too. It's going to be an interesting year.

After the ceremony, an American officer approaches me. He is from the public affairs department here—an office that we have endeavoured to cultivate a close relationship with. 'Hey Josh,' he says, 'I cannot tell you what exactly it is, but be prepared to go down to Helmand next week. Something big is about to happen.' Puzzled, yet intrigued, I begin to make the necessary arrangements. All I know at this stage is that it involves the newly arrived US Marines—who are part of the surge force—and that it will be happening soon.

THURSDAY 18 JUNE

I have started to meet up with three Americans that attend the chapel: Brian, Tonya, and Charles. Brian and Tonya are in the US Air Force, and Charles is a civilian who helps teach English to Afghan pilots. We meet in Brian's room every day to study the Bible. This is my first major contact with other Christians since arriving out here last year. We talk, laugh, and pray together, and I am very grateful that God has given me these people.

SUNDAY 21 JUNE

During the service tonight, Wes appeals for help from any who are able to assist in the running of the chapel in any way. Before I can catch myself, I find myself volunteering to preach. Josh, what are you doing? I've never preached before, and already I am terrified at the prospect of standing up and talking in front of other people. I try to arrange a date to preach with Wes: it's hard to know how long this 'thing' in Helmand will run for, so we tentatively agree on a Sunday in mid-August.

MONDAY 22 JUNE

In our nightly Bible study Brian, Tonya, Charles and I look at the example of King Hezekiah. Hezekiah was one of the kings of Judah—from a long line of rather bad apples who repeatedly turned from God and committed great acts of evil. Occasionally, one would briefly turn back to God, but wouldn't have the moral strength to remove all the evil idols in the land. Hezekiah adopted a different approach—'no compromise'—and set about removing every offending idol and place of false worship in his realm, dedicating the land solely to God.

We all feel challenged. It's often that we can be tempted to be like Hezekiah's predecessors—not quite wanting to root out everything in our lives that can harm our relationship with God—and because of that, we can miss out on some of God's blessings. I realize that there are several habits in my own life that I am holding onto despite my desire to be close to God, that are not helpful. I resolve to stop them, realising that this is only possible if I trust in God—a milestone in the mature development of a Christian.

TUESDAY 23 JUNE

Attend a brief at HQ regarding the upcoming Helmand operation. A host of ambassadors arrive, and listen as General McChrystal begins to outline the plan. It seems there is indeed going to be a big shift here—we are moving away from conventional war-fighting and adopting a policy known as 'COIN', or Counter Insurgency. COIN was used in Iraq in 2007, and many have attributed the rapid drop in insurgent-related activity there to its adoption. The fundamental rule of COIN is to make the focus 'winning the population over by protecting them and providing security' rather than chasing down insurgents and unleashing as much firepower as possible on them. McChrystal, his eyes shining with conviction, explains that if the populations of the various towns and villages in Helmand feel secure, their livelihoods and overall quality of life will increase, and before long they will be rejecting the Taliban of their own volition. However, if ISAF soldiers go in, all guns blazing, dropping bombs on compounds, then we will alienate the population, and the coveted bubble of security will never be created. A new moniker is created: 'courageous restraint', a term designed for soldiers who decide not to use airstrikes or artillery on compounds that the enemy are firing at them from, and choose to withdraw instead to prevent any civilian casualties. It is a noble idea, but I suspect that it will not sit well with the front line troops who will be soaking up the enemy fire. If this idea came from the lips of anyone but McChrystal, I don't imagine that it would go very far, but because of his Special Forces background, he *might* just have the credibility to pull this off.

The plan will be to drop over four thousand US Marines into parts of southern Helmand—Nawa, Garmsir, and Khan Neshin. It will be the largest Marine air assault since Vietnam. Once on the ground, the Marines will seek to push the Taliban back from town centres, and begin to implement COIN techniques.

WEDNESDAY 24 JUNE

10.00 p.m.—Fly down to Helmand. Am slightly surprised to see no Marines waiting to pick me up. I trudge over to the British area, and call them. There has been an error with communications, and the Marines didn't have any idea that I was coming down. Ah.

THURSDAY 25 JUNE

7.00 a.m.—Wake up, and begin to try and sort out this mess. I email the Marines, begging them to find a space for me. I ask officers in Kabul to pull strings and to extol the virtues of taking me on.

9.00 p.m.—After a day of frantic emails and begging, the Marines finally agree to have me. A British press officer drives me over to the Marine part of Bastion—a whole new section called Camp Leatherneck. Dust-coloured tents, vehicles, and barbed wire adorn the sandy domain of the Marines. Their press officer, Bill, puts me in a tent with several other journalists. It seems that all the big players in print, television and radio are here. Whatever is happening here is going to be big. Bill pulls us all out and speaks to us. He is a gruff, old school Marine who barely attempts to disguise his contempt for the media. Verbal sparring between him and other journalists—several of whom are extremely witty—ensues, to muted hilarity.

There is no word on when D-Day itself will happen yet, as they don't want the information slipping out to the wider world. Seeing that I am a latecomer, I imagine that my chances of getting on the helicopter assault will be fairly limited, but I will see what I can do. I have resolved that on this operation, I will not be playing the guessing/worrying game of whether I am going to get what I need—I am simply going to trust God and see what happens.

FRIDAY 26 JUNE

A US Navy cameraman called Dave arrives from Kabul. I have seen him several times in various meetings at HQ. Dave is moving to a forward base tomorrow, and I ask if I can go with him—I feel that my chances of taking part in the operation are probably in direct correlation with how far I can get away from Bill.

SATURDAY 27 JUNE

7.00 p.m.—At the Bastion HLS, waiting for a flight to FOB Dwyer. My heart sank when I found out that I would be returning to Dwyer. It is the singularly grimmest base I have seen in Afghanistan thus far, an unforgiving heat sink that roasts people and saps morale. I foster a secret hope that facilities have perhaps improved there—it's a year since I was last at Dwyer—but I remember that the custodians of the camp, the US Marine Corps, are not big on creature comforts, and draw a certain pride from roughing it, in direct contrast to their brothers in the Army, Air Force, and Navy.

Traveling with me are Graham, an American radio journalist; Rajiv, a well-known author who works for the Washington Post; and Dave. Relieved to be escaping from Leatherneck, everybody talks excitedly as we board the helicopter. Expectation hangs heavily in the air.

1.00 p.m.—Arrive at FOB Dwyer. I think it's even hotter than last time, despite the darkness. The camp is certainly bigger: rows and rows of dusty-coloured tents loom in the darkness. Put in a tent with semi-functional air conditioning. The cooling part does not work, but the fan does. Bombarded with hot air all night.

SUNDAY 28 JUNE

It's hot and bright in Dwyer. Moon dust everywhere, still. This is definitely one of my least favourite places on Earth. Slog my way to and from the large tent that serves as a dining facility. Sweat drips from the end of noses, swallowed up immediately by the parched ground.

We are placed with different Marine units today; everybody hoping that they are the ones to take part in the air assault. Dave and I, being the only cameras here at this time, have to decide who gets to go by helicopter, and who comes in a ground convoy, crawling in somewhat less gloriously, several days after the main assault. Dave graciously concedes, and lets me go—after all, we are working to the same goal, and NATO TV probably has a slightly larger coverage worldwide than the US combat camera teams. Very excited. As far as I know, I am one of the only cameras in the world that will be taking part in this gargantuan air assault. Begin to harbour panic-ridden thoughts of inadvertently committing video suicide by forgetting to charge the batteries, running out of tape, or shooting a historic moment with the lens cap still on.

3.00 p.m.—Trudge over to meet the Marines that I will be inserting with. They are housed in two massive tents; sweaty, dirty, and raring to go like young sportsmen approaching the big game. I meet some brilliant military stereotypes. There is the tough talking, fierce African-American first sergeant (or sergeant major in British terms), and the laconic, tobacco-chewing gunnery sergeant, hailing from one of the Southern states. He carries a shotgun around with him like a baby. And of course, there are the young, inexperienced Marines, for whom this will be the first taste of combat. I see them sitting on their beds, talking to their friends, and behind their stares lies barely hidden apprehension, excitement, fear.

A Marine lieutenant named Oliver introduces himself to me. I will be in his chalk on the helicopter. A 'chalk' is an American term used to denote the people that are on the helicopter, and what order they will be touching down. We will be in the second chalk, and therefore will be touching down just after the first chalk.

Oliver and I go for a run with all our equipment on—I suspect that he is angling to see what sort of physical calibre I possess, and whether I will be a burden to his platoon. Thankfully, due to a rather physical summer, combined with lots of running back in Kabul, I am able to finish before him by quite some way. I do suspect, however, that his burden weighs far more than mine. He is instantly warm to me afterwards; military folks are definitely governed by 'respect through physical means', and I find that I am soon ingratiated in his platoon. If only all my embeds could start off with a run!

MONDAY 29 JUNE

Marines are patrolling round Dwyer, fine-tuning their tactics and techniques for the upcoming operation. I have never seen such anticipation for an operation before. This must be a slice of what preparing for D-Day in World War Two must have been like. I am very thankful that I am here, I don't think I will ever experience something like this again. Trying not to think about possible combat scenarios that will involve my injury or demise.

TUESDAY 30 JUNE

The Marines from Oliver's platoon are called together for a talk with their commanding officer. He outlines to them where they (and by inclusion, me) will be going: a village called Sorkh-Duz, which is south of Nawa. Instantly my heart begins to pump. Nawa was where Jon was shot, and I was involved in the frantic rescue in March. Nawa, the hive of Taliban activity. This could get really bad.

The commanding officer begins to make a final speech to his men. D-Day is expected to be tomorrow night, and the Marines will spend most of the day tomorrow resting. His talk reminds me of the type of epic, inspirational speech that only seem to exist on the silver screen. He tells his men that they are about to become part of history, that they will remember what they do over the next few days for the rest of their lives, that this operation could be the beginning of victory in Afghanistan. Despite the goose pimples rising on my skin—these are certainly very stirring words—

I force myself to listen with a pinch of salt. Will the flood of Marines about to pour into southern Helmand really change the game here? Will McChrystal's COIN strategy really work? 'This is the largest operation ever launched by ISAF forces,' says the commander, 'and the largest Marine air assault since Vietnam. This is history, gentlemen.' There is a reverent silence. I look around. Some of the Marines are no older than eighteen, and yet are now shouldered with the burden of rescuing the Afghan campaign.

3.00 p.m.—Everybody taking part in the air assault assembles on a vast piece of desert next to the tents. We line up in our chalks, and practice the order of embarkation, as well as dismounting. It's quite hard to imagine whirring helicopters and possible enemy resistance in this serene, breezy desert. I find myself crouched next to a young Marine called Paul. He has a large black dog named Jag. It's Jag's job to find any bombs. Paul tells me that sometimes he has to order Jag to run up and down a road, searching for bombs. Inevitably, some dogs like this set off bombs themselves. While this is unfortunate, if it's a choice between a dog or Marine, most would choose the animal. Looking at Jag's big brown eyes and playful expression, I do find myself hoping that he doesn't step on anything that he shouldn't. Paul asks me about combat: he has never experienced it, but is excited at the prospect. I inwardly chuckle—I am seeing a reflection of myself one year ago. I describe my experiences to him, inwardly supposing that I have somehow become a combat veteran of sorts.

7.00 p.m.—Sit on a box watching the sunset, praying. I have no idea what the next few days will hold. I am certain that people will die on this operation—but who, and how many, remain to be seen. I wonder how I would cope if I lost my legs? To my great shame, I think I'd prefer just to die outright.

WEDNESDAY 1 JULY

Mission launch tonight. I spend the day packing my bags and resting. I need to carry several days' worth of food and water in addition to all my equipment, and my load is crushing, even compared to what I carried on Op Mar Lewe. I try not to think what I will do if we get ambushed as we exit the helicopter: I would probably be able to move with the speed of a snail under the beak of a crow.

6.00 p.m.—Hundreds of Marines form up and begin to march toward FOB Dwyer HLS. Not all of the four thousand will be launching from here; some will be flying from Leatherneck and one or two other bases. Some will be driving.

I step out of the marching column and begin to film the seemingly endless line of dusty Marines. The sun is beginning to set, casting an orange light on everything—it's a picturesque moment of relative calm. The Marines reach the HLS. We will be sleeping under the stars tonight, and the operation will be commencing at dawn tomorrow. In the gathering darkness, officers call their soldiers together for a final chat. They remind the men to remember courageous restraint. Inadvertently blowing up a family of civilians that the Taliban are using as human shields will not further ISAF goals here.

I conduct some final interviews, then bed down under the hard light of the stars. Few people sleep. We are caked in fine dust, and far too nervous about the next day's events to even close our eyes. An Afghan interpreter sits near me, and we begin to talk. He is an intelligent young man, who asks me to call him Jason. Many of the 'terps' here have given themselves Western names to make it easier for the Marines. Jason talks about his wife, who is up north in Kabul, and how hard it is to be separated from her. His plan is to earn as much money down here as he can, and then emigrate to America. Many of the interpreters I meet harbour the same ambitions. Jason has worked with both the British and American soldiers throughout the country for several years, and it's likely he has seen more combat than most of the people sitting underneath the open sky tonight. He asks me about how I feel in combat, whether I get scared or not. I answer that I do, but that I trust in God. Not insofar as to think that he will make me invincible, but along the lines of the promise in the Bible that 'all things work together for the good of those that love God'. Even if I am shot, blown up, or injured in

The first of the helicopters touches down in Dwyer. Over the next few hours, hundreds of Marines will be dropped throughout Helmand.

some other way, I know that God is doing it for my ultimate good, even if I do not understand it at the time.

THURSDAY 2 JULY

4.00 a.m.—I wake before the majority of the sleeping Marines. The promise of dawn infuses the sky. It is an impressive sight: almost one thousand sleeping bodies lying in the dust under a deep blue sky, ready to fly into danger. This is it. I check my equipment—everything is good to go. The Marines begin to wake. There is no washing to do, no clothes to change into; everyone is ready.

5.00 a.m.—The first low thump of approaching helicopters can be heard. In the sky, four Marine choppers—dark silhouettes against the slowly lightening sky—gracefully descend toward us. Once again, I can't escape how cinematic this all is, how removed from mundane reality the scenes before me are. I feel very privileged to bear witness to the spectacle.

The helicopters touch down in a perfect line. Columns of Marines—ordered in their chalks—begin to run toward the open doors of the helicopters. Oliver signals to us and my column begins to take off at a brisk pace. I hit 'record' on the camera, and jog along behind the Marines. To the right and the left of us, other chalks run toward their designated vehicles. It is a breathtaking sight. Up the ramp, into the belly of the beast. We do not remove our backpacks—this is going to be a hot insertion, Taliban might be lying in wait, and we need to get out of the helicopter as quickly as possible. The speed of the rotors increases, and we are airborne. The noise is deafening—every man is lost in his own thoughts, surrounded by comrades, yet totally alone. Marines exchange looks. A young guy opposite me exhales fiercely; puffing his cheeks out like a boxer about to fight. My heart begins to beat faster, harder. A message is passed down the line; the simple gesture of two fingers being held up. Two minutes until landing. 'Whump whump whump' go the rotors. 'Thump thump thump' goes my heart. Is there going to be a firefight as we land? Am I going to have to struggle down the ramp into enemy fire and hope for the best? One minute. The helicopter begins to bank and swerve, flying low and fast to deter any RPGs fired from the Taliban. Suddenly we can feel ourselves descending. Out the rear door, I can see long grass swaying violently in the downdraft from the helicopter. Touch down. Marines begin to pile out. I see Jag, the black dog, faithfully pulling Paul out, straining at his lead, undaunted by the noise and force of the chopper. Operation Khanjar—which means 'strike of the sword'—has started.

I stumble off the helicopter. Jason is in front of me and, in typical Afghan fashion, he has tied some gaudy blankets and pillows to his backpack. It's not quite the shot I wanted: a big, colourful, comfortable-looking bag running off the back ramp of a Marine helicopter. In the long grass, I throw myself against a bank, beside a Marine with a machine gun who is already scanning the nearby building of Sorkh Duz to check for any Taliban threat. The last Marines exit the helicopter and it lifts off, lashing the grass in violent ripples and pelting us with dust. Then it is gone. Silence descends. The grass swishes softly in the breeze as it returns to its original position. A distant rooster crows. Locals peer out from windows and doorways at the Marines sitting in a field beside their village. I can't help but feel like I have taken part in a massive, orchestrated anticlimax. Judging by the looks of some of the Marines around me, I think they are feeling the same thing. Most of us, it seems, were expecting a D-Day-esque charge into heavy enemy fire. I can't decide whether I am relieved or slightly disappointed.

9.00 a.m.—We have been sitting in this field for a while now. Captain Sun, the Marine company commander, is negotiating with a local farmer: he wants his Marines to live in one of the compounds of the village, and this farmer, after negotiation over fees, is happy let the Marines rent out his place. Living with the population—as opposed to being stuck away in a base somewhere—is a key element of COIN tactics, and the Marines here, despite the anticlimax, are keen to get stuck into their mission.

The temperature is beginning to rise. I remember how hot it was on Mar Lewe. I suspect that it's going to be the same here—maybe even worse, because we're further south.

12.00 noon—Move into the farmer's place. Another dusty compound. I begin to feel my morale plummeting. It's going to be a hot, sweaty, tiresome operation—and the only glimmer of excitement seems to be fading.

Captain Sun goes out on a patrol into the village to meet the elders; white-bearded wrinkly men who squint at us through tired eyes, asking for wells, clinics and schools. Captain Sun pulls out a notepad and begins to write down their requests, 'promising to see what he could do'. It's at this moment, as I film the exchange, sweating pouring from underneath my helmet, that my resolution begins to waver. Over the last fifteen months, I have attended many meetings with elders; I have heard many promises made and, judging from what I have seen and later learnt, precious few are kept. It also seems that the Afghans—used to various foreigners in their land throughout the years—are not overly interested in cooperation, simply keen to see what they can get from the deal. I begin to question myself. I think that the idea of trying to help the Afghan people and bring peace is a good concept … but I am not entirely sure if it is achievable.

5.00 p.m.—We hear reports over the radio that the Marine company to the south of us has been involved in heavy fighting, and has taken several casualties. I can see the Marines here begin to itch with frustration at not being in the fight with their friends, yet they remain professional and committed to their COIN efforts here, as unglamorous as they may be.

FRIDAY 3 JULY

Being very entertainment-light, having sacrificed the prospect of extra books or gadgets to accommodate food and water, my sole source of escapism is my Bible. As I open it, I am struck by how much I have viewed reading it as a chore throughout the years. Even during the spiritual highs, there has always the faint nagging sense that it is a 'duty' to read the Bible. While it is good for a reader to adopt a scholarly attitude toward it—seeking to extract an application from the text—I now challenge myself to try and really enjoy it too. There are so many stories in there of incredible people who went through such a variety of life-changing events including wars, conflicts, and suffering. I begin to read, putting myself in the shoes of the great warriors, kings, and generals that the Bible describes. Story after story passes, and I realize that my knowledge of the Bible is far less than it should be. I have long been dining off the fact that I have grown up in a Christian family, and regularly attended church. I haven't made it personal. I haven't made it mine. As I read, I am struck by the stories of those who had to overcome particularly difficult or dangerous circumstances. Take David and Goliath, for example. I know the story so well—we all do—that Goliath's defeat and subsequent demise never seems in doubt. I try to imagine what it must have been like to be David, walking towards a massive bloke in heavy armour, equipped with nothing but a sling and a few stones. That requires serious bravery and trust in God. I ask God to help me to be like these incredible men and women—people who, despite difficulties, never wavered in their trust of him.

2.00 p.m.—Go on a patrol with the Marines. We find an abandoned, partially destroyed old school building. Afghan graffiti adorns the walls;

crudely drawn images of stick men shooting down helicopters and blowing up tanks with rockets. Despite the blazing afternoon heat, it's slightly chilling. Meet more elders, hear more grievances, make more promises.

SATURDAY 4 JULY

Captain Sun and his first sergeant resolve to make American Independence Day as special as they can for their Marines, despite the unpleasant conditions. They are able to secure some local bread—Afghan bread being, in my opinion, the best bread on earth—and a roasted goat. We are even given cans of warm orange soda sourced from an enterprising Afghan. Being British, I feel slightly traitorous for partaking of this, but after several days of cheerless US-issue rations, it is a culinary feast.

More patrols. Sweaty. Dusty.

SUNDAY 5 JULY

Some other journalists begin to arrive in the road convoy today. The Marines care little for extra media, but they are glad to have more supplies which, until now, have been dropped off by a helicopter—always a risky operation.

TUESDAY 7 JULY

My work in this area is done. I have filmed as many quiet patrols and elders as I can stand, and it's now time to go back to Kabul to begin editing stories. I wish the Marines all the best with the rest of their tour—they are great guys, and cheerful in the face of hardships that many people in the military would not be able to stomach. As I walk to my chariot, a heavily armoured vehicle, I bid a silent and unloving goodbye to the makeshift toilet that we have all used for the last few days: a wooden ammunition box that one has to squat on to 'go' into a sticky plastic bag. Goodbye, you splinter-filled cube of joy.

WEDNESDAY 8 JULY

At the British and American base in Garmsir. The convoy dropped me here last night. From here, I will seek to go back to FOB Dwyer—oh the joy—and onward to Leatherneck, then Kabul. I think I have become slightly dehydrated over the last week, and slightly deranged; for a moment I consider walking on my own to Dwyer—over 30km of Afghan desert—as a viable way to travel onward. I am glad this doesn't happen. In my tent are two Marines that were evacuated from the fighting to the south of us on the first day of the operation. They describe to me how they were pinned down from the rest of the company, the incoming fire from the Taliban so accurate they were unable to move over to their comrades to get any more water. They soon collapsed from heat exhaustion, and had to be evacuated. A brave Marine pilot flew in to rescue them, but a rocket from the Taliban flew just over its rotor blades as the stricken men were loaded aboard. A close call. That would have made incredible footage.

SATURDAY 11 JULY

Finally back in Kabul. Was able to send footage of the operation off as soon as I returned to Bastion. Thomas has emailed me, ecstatic; television networks all over the world have used my footage from the air assault, and it's good to know that all the effort and sweat was worth it.

SUNDAY 19 JULY

My first sermon tonight at church. Terrified. I am preaching from 2 Peter. The sermon title is 'Being Productive in Christ'. I look at my watch as the hours tick by—far too quickly—until it is seven o'clock. At church, we sing the hymns and songs, then, with a big smile, Wes calls me up. Knees knocking, and absolutely convinced that this is more terrifying than getting shot at, I walk to the front and begin to preach. I spent about twenty hours writing this sermon—most of which was working out how on earth to write and structure such a talk—but, like a meal that takes ages to prepare and is finished all too quickly, I am done before I know it. The feedback is good—although I suspect that people are trying to be as kind as possible. Charles, the English teacher, comes up and slaps me on the back. 'Well done, bro. You did vomit it all out quickly though!' That would be the nerves, then. Must slow down next time. It was absolutely thrilling, though. I really, really enjoyed preaching. Ask Wes if I can do it again, soon.

WEDNESDAY 22 JULY

I am beginning to worry about going bald. It is hereditary in my family, and I can see the first signs of hair loss beginning to take effect, as follicles give up the ghost like cheap lights failing on a Christmas tree. I reckon I have about five or six years, maybe more, until I begin to resemble an egg. The problem is that I am single and, being pretty much permanently stuck out here, the chances of meeting a potential wife are pretty small. After the various things that I have gone to God about over the last few months, I do feel slightly silly asking about this, but it feels quite important to me. Like everything else that I have been through with him recently, I resolve to leave this entirely with God. He knows what is best for me, and if he wants to provide me with a wife, he is more than able to do so. Even so, every time I get out of the shower, I look at my hair in the mirror and fight the urge to fret.

THURSDAY 23 JULY

8.00 a.m.—While running round the Kabul airbase in the morning, I see a dead dog trapped in the razor wire that covers a small drainage tunnel running underneath the road, depositing waste water outside the base. The razor wire is in place to prevent any enterprising Taliban from gaining access to the airfield. Evidently, the poor dog entered the tunnel, tried to get through the razor wire, but eventually succumbed to the numerous cuts and heat. An awful way to go.

3.00 p.m.—Driving back from an errand on the northern side of the airport. As I pass the sewage tunnel, I see movement. I pull over and look.

The dog is moving. Cursing my stupidity at not checking properly this morning, I dash back to my accommodation—I am going to need help to do this. Will is in our room, and agrees to come and help me. We haven't got any wire cutters and, even if we did, it wouldn't be a good idea for us to disable the defences of a rather vulnerable part of the base. Arrive back at the tunnel. The dog is about two meters into the wire, surrounded by sewage, and rescuing him is going to take some time. Step by step, ankle deep in the foul-smelling bog, Will and I painstakingly inch toward him. We wear our body armour and gloves. Needless to say, all our clothes sustain numerous small rips. We are able to work the wire free of the dog, although several barbs are embedded fairly deep in his body. Thinking back wistfully to the analogy of the bear, the trap and the ranger, I imagine that usually a dog would be furious at anyone causing such pain, but this fellow seems to have completely given up on life. After about an hour of work, he is almost free. We shout at him to make a final push through to us, since he is such a large dog that lifting him from where he is would be impossible. Sensing our urgency, and the possibility of freedom, the dog stands to his shaky legs and throws himself forward, clearing the wire and collapsing in a heap. I pick him up like a baby, and we take him to the car. We are unsure what to do—if military police see us with him, they will demand that he is taken away and shot; he could carry numerous diseases. We resolve, therefore, to drive outside the base and set him free. We place him in the boot of the car, and drive out of the gate.

We find a quiet bit of shade by a stream, and unload him. He seems to have regained some strength, and is able to walk, albeit painfully. We watch him go, like concerned parents. Will gives him the name 'Jobin'. 'Goodbye, Jobin,' we say, not without emotion, as our new friend limps off into the sunset.

Will and I celebrate the successful rescue with our usual evening custom: buying a two-foot long watermelon from some local Afghans, and eating out of it with a spoon while watching a movie.

FRIDAY 7 AUGUST

Charles invites me to attend an underground church in Kabul with him today. Friday being the Afghan equivalent of Sunday here, the ex-pats who run the church—which is for foreigners only—decide to hold it on a Friday morning. Charles and I take a taxi into the city, and then walk the rest of the way. It is a secretive affair—the location changes every week—and by the time we have walked through the maze of small roads, I have no idea where we are.

The service—which is packed with about fifty lightly sweating white people—begins, like church services back home, with notices. The only difference is, where the notices back home might involve informing the congregation that 'there will be a Bible study here on Wednesday', the information given here is a tad more immediate. 'If gunmen come in shooting,' we are told, 'run out this way…' It's the first time I have heard a service begin with words like that. We begin to sing—and despite the fact that we are all fairly out of tune, and there is only one guitar, the experience is like nothing I have seen or heard before. It can be so easy in church back home to only half-sing the words of the songs, and for the singing to become just a habit all too easily. Here, in this city, it feels completely different. Despite the potential peril of meeting like this, everybody is filled with a real sense of joy at being able to meet and praise God. The atmosphere is incredible. Charles turns to me. 'This is what heaven is going to sound like,' he says.

SATURDAY 15 AUGUST

As I complete my morning workout, there is a distant BANG! that makes the walls vibrate. Bomb. Everybody dashes outside to look for the telltale mushroom cloud. There it is, rising slowly in the sky, several kilometres away. Reports begin to filter through that HQ has been hit. Mel and I jump in a taxi and drive over there. 'Ambulance chasing'—the media practice of turning up at disasters and filming the destruction—is not entirely what we want to do, but it will be necessary for us to record the official ISAF statement and release it to the world's media.

We arrive at the scene of the blast. It was a huge explosion. Concrete blocks, each weighing several tones, have been flipped over. All the windows of the large Afghan building opposite HQ have been destroyed.

Blood cakes the shattered ground. Parts of a vehicle, twisted and burnt beyond recognition, are scattered everywhere. Here and there are ragged pieces of flesh. At the epicentre of the blast—a sight I will never forget—lie the charred genitalia of the suicide bomber, the only part of him that is left. A bomb-disposal officer explains that at the time of the blast, these suicide bombers will often clasp their groin with one hand and detonate with the other. They are keen to keep their male members for the afterlife, where they believe they will receive their seventy-two virgins for martyring themselves. At least seven people—all Afghans—are dead. Ninety-one injured. What a waste of life.

MONDAY 20 JULY

Back in Helmand. Big day. It's the polling for the Afghan presidential election. The build-up to this has been making headlines in the world's media. The incumbent President, Hamid Karzai, is facing challenges from over forty other candidates. Some are no-hopers, but one or two may prove to be worthy adversaries. His administration has been frequently mired in allegations of corruption, and there are some who privately are hoping that he is replaced. The Taliban have promised to create havoc today, vowing to kill Afghans who come forward to vote, and they have threatened to attack polling stations.

Will the Afghans vote, or will they stay away? Will the bloodshed during operations to try and secure population centres prove to be worth it? I am down here to try and record some answers.

ISAF forces are trying to stay clear of the polling stations—having the Afghan police and army there will create the 'Afghan face' to the security that is desired—and thus I am rather limited in my choice of polling stations. A British major named Ric, one of the press officers on Bastion, kindly rescues my day by taking me to a polling station designed for the Afghan army, and then a smaller one for locals living just outside Camp Bastion. Each voter is required to dip their finger in so-called indelible ink, and place their mark next to the candidate of their choice.

Throughout the country, there are reports of widespread violence. In Kandahar, the Taliban hang two Afghans whose fingers are stained with ink. Two American soldiers are killed by a bomb in the eastern part of Afghanistan, one British soldier dies in Helmand. In total, there are more than 400 attacks today, making it one of the most violent days in Afghanistan since the fall of the Taliban in 2001. The question hangs in the air—will all the violence be worth it? Will allegations of corruption —rife throughout the weeks preceding this election—prove to be true? We won't know until October.

10 Mountains, Hills, and Valleys

5 September 2009—4 December 2009

SATURDAY 5 SEPTEMBER

Back home in the UK on leave. Decide to visit the new pastor of our church today. We have been pastorless for a couple of years after my Dad was called by God to work full-time in prison chaplaincy and Don, the new pastor, is living in the church house that we used to live in.

I ring the bell. A beautiful girl with dark hair and brown eyes answers the door. She introduces herself as Danielle, Don's daughter. Like me, she has only recently returned to God having fallen away from the church for a period of time. The catalyst that brought her back to God was the shock of an unplanned pregnancy and, now seeking to honour him, she has decided to keep the baby despite the stigma, financial challenge, and uncertain future as a single mother that such a decision brings. The baby is due in March.

I sit with Don, his wife Melody, and Danielle, and tell them about myself and my work in Afghanistan. They seem like a nice family.

FRIDAY 18 SEPTEMBER

In Greece. I have spent the last week in Australia visiting a friend, and I wanted to make a short detour through Greece on the way back to the UK. For several years, I have been fascinated by the story of the three hundred Spartans who made a desperate last stand against the overwhelming might of Xerxes' Persian army. I have planned a brief 'pilgrimage' of sorts to Thermopylae, the place where the battle was fought, and where the Spartans were finally overwhelmed by the arrows of the Persians.

My Greek friend and host, Ioannis, gives me rough directions to Thermopylae. I board a coach, and after a few hours and a dodgy taxi ride, I am there. A large bronze statue of King Leonidas—the Spartan king—stands, overlooking the battlefield. There is a large mound where the Spartans made their final stand. Upon the pinnacle of the hill is a plaque, with Greek script engraved on it. It translates as:

'Go tell the Spartans, thou who passest by,
That here, obedient to their laws, we lie.'

So many arrows were fired at the Spartans on this hill, that metal arrowheads were being discovered fairly regularly for many centuries after the battle. The romanticized idea that it was just three hundred Spartans has been disproven by history—there were a number of Greek soldiers from other armies who also joined in. The fact remains, however, that the defenders were hopelessly outnumbered. I sit on the hill as the breeze gently caresses the grass, the blazing hot sun sapping strength, and the local insects buzzing lazily above my head. I try to imagine what it must have been like for the Greeks. What bravery must have been in the hearts of those men, willing to fight to their assured death, in order to fulfil their code of honour, and to delay the Persians as long as possible.

Feeling moved, I open my Bible to Romans, and a verse jumps out at me from chapter 12:

'Therefore, I urge you, brothers and sisters, in view of God's mercy, to offer your bodies as a living sacrifice, holy and pleasing to God...' (Romans 12:1)

The idea of sacrifice—which seems to ebb from the earth, trees, and mountains of Thermopylae—strongly resonates in my mind. That same bravery, that same selflessness: that is how, as Christians, God wants us to live. But instead of one final act of sacrifice—like the Spartans here—the Christian's sacrifice, a 'living sacrifice', should be a daily occurrence, when our hopes, our goals, our desires, our words, and our thoughts are constantly re-evaluated in the light of putting God and other people first.

I trudge back down the hill, humbled at what I have seen.

MONDAY 5 OCTOBER

Back in Afghanistan. Preparing to go into the western mountains with US paratroopers; it will be nice to have a small break from all the trips to Helmand I have done this year.

I add Danielle, the new pastor's daughter, on Facebook. We talk briefly. Chat via the Internet is always a blessing to me—I have never been very good speaking to girls, especially attractive ones, and the Internet allows me to make up for my shyness.

SATURDAY 10 OCTOBER

In the mountains of Herat with soldiers from the US 82nd Airborne Division. This is different from my last few trips to this province, with no luxury lobster or comfortable bed in sight. I commit one of the cardinal sins of bag packing and, completely used to Helmand, do not bring much warm clothing. We are very high above sea level, and as the sun sinks I am reduced to a gibbering wreck. The US soldiers have a quick whip round for warm gear, and are able to adequately provide for me. They have taken me to their hearts since I traded them several British paratrooper badges yesterday—it's fascinating how paratroopers, serving or former, always instantly bond, regardless of nationality, with one another. I think that the shared experience of throwing oneself out of an airplane with nothing but a thin sheet of canvas making the difference between life and death is an astonishing leveller.

As I dig my bed for the night into the mountainside, I find a massive camel spider. I have heard legends about these beasts for several years in both Iraq and Afghanistan, but this is the first time I have laid eyes on one. They are mythologised for their bite, which is said to anesthetise the area of skin around the wound, allowing them to gnaw away with razor-sharp mandibles completely unbeknownst to the subject of their feast. True or not, they look like something out of a nightmare. Relentlessly grim. The fact that I have found one where I am about to sleep does not go down well with anyone. The soldiers throw the spider into the fire, and begin to search around for any others. Nobody wants to become dinner tonight.

Spend the night tossing and turning, imagining arthropod intruders crawling all over my sleeping bag.

SUNDAY 11 OCTOBER

In this bleak mountain outpost, there is not much to do. The wind howls constantly; everybody talks through chapped lips. The soldiers have adopted a sheep, which they have named Delilah. While wartime pets are fairly common, this is the first time that I have seen soldiers take a sheep into their midst. I catch some Afghan troops—who are also based here—repeatedly eyeing Delilah hungrily.

5.00 p.m.—On the way back from an exhausting patrol around the mountains. I am quite impressed by the Afghans: they exhibit a natural grace and agility as they bound up the steep slopes, leaving the Americans and I panting in their wake. It could be, however, due to the fact that they are not wearing over twenty-five kilograms of gear.

We finally make it back to the mountain outpost. Despite the rising cold, we are all sweating. 'Hey,' an American soldier calls, 'where's Delilah?' We look around. No sign of her. A thin line of smoke rises from the Afghan tent beneath us. Ah.

About twenty minutes later, a beaming Afghan chef walks up toward us with a large plate of sizzling meat and Afghan bread. Feeling slightly guilty, but famished after the patrol, we begin to tuck in. 'Sorry, Delilah,' the guy next to me says through a mouthful of meat, 'but man, you taste good.'

TUESDAY 12 OCTOBER

US troops—in conjunction with Afghan police and army—launch a small patrol into a small village today to try and root out an alleged pocket of Taliban resistance who have taken up there. The Afghan police take the lead—quite ponderously, we feel—and it takes some time to move through the alleyways and compounds. The Taliban, of course, have long since fled, but the Afghans find a weapons cache, containing rifles, rockets, and grenades. If nothing else, the Taliban in this area will be toothless for a while.

I was told that we would be out doing this for a matter of hours, and we would then return to the primary base in Herat. Once again, I foolishly pack based on an incorrect assumption, and am kicking myself when, almost inevitably, the message comes through that we are to stay out for several days. One of these days, I will finally learn my lesson.

MONDAY 19 OCTOBER

Back in Kabul. I phone home, and find out from Dad, who has heard from my grandmother who, in turn, has heard from Danielle's mum that Danielle enjoyed speaking to me on Facebook. Instant flare of hope. There's no way that she could like me, is there?

TUESDAY 3 NOVEMBER

Mel is bitten by a dog while she is down in Kandahar. There are concerns that the wound might be infected, and therefore she graciously lets me have her upcoming trip to the districts of Sangin and Kajaki in Helmand. Sangin has been the most deadly area for British troops in recent months—the Taliban activity around there is frenetic, and many, many lives and limbs have been lost during action there. I am excited, yet understandably apprehensive about going there, especially now that the prospect of combat has lost its shine. I am flying down there at some stage next week.

SATURDAY 7 NOVEMBER

Tomorrow is Remembrance Sunday in the UK. I email a letter back to my church:

'As a man who is working in Afghanistan, who has seen soldiers wounded and maimed this year—and then witnessed their colleagues risk life and limb to save them—the idea of remembrance resonates strongly inside me. In life, people don't often get the choice of how, where, or why they die. But some place themselves in situations where death lurks with every step that they take. I have seen the look in the eyes of an 18-year old soldier preparing to go out on patrol, knowing that he may not return from it—it is a profound and deeply moving thing to see. Even as you read this letter, there are soldiers out on patrol, or preparing to go out on patrol in Afghanistan, where they may well be killed by a bullet or bomb.

The sacrifices that those who are serving, and those who have served in the Armed Forces are willing to make is humbling—and as we see thousands of poppies displayed over the UK today, we are reminded of the hundreds of thousands of soldiers, airmen, sailors, and marines who gave their lives as an act of sacrifice to their country. In John 15:13, Jesus says 'Greater love has no one than this, to lay down one's life for one's friends'. The laying down of one's life for their country, their friends, and their loved ones is a supreme act of love—a reflection of the love that Christ had for us, a love that was demonstrated in the fact that 'While we were still sinners, Christ died for us'. Today, as we think upon the sacrifices that so many made for our country, let us remember the sacrifice that Christ made for our souls.

In humble remembrance with you,

Josh'

SUNDAY 9 NOVEMBER

Preach in the chapel tonight. I am slowly getting more comfortable with the business of public speaking. We close by singing 'Amazing Grace'. I have fallen deeply in love with one of the verses that reads:

'Through many dangers, toils and snares,
we have already come.
'Twas Grace that brought us safe thus far,
and Grace will lead us home.'

I don't think there are many things that sum up my Afghan experience thus far as well as this one. When I arrived here nineteen months ago, my heart was far from God.

FRIDAY 13 NOVEMBER

Riding on a Chinook up to Kajaki, where I will be spending a week or so before heading to Sangin. Kajaki is the home of the famous dam in Helmand, which was built in 1953 by an American construction firm. Water from the dam flows down to form the great Helmand River, which I have encountered in various places further south in the Province during my travels—Gereshk, Nadi Ali, Nawa, and Garmsir. Control of the dam is of great strategic importance, as it supplies electricity as well as water, and therefore there is a whole company of infantry stationed there to protect the dam from any Taliban attacks.

The Chinook banks low over a vast, vibrant, shining blue lake. I have never seen anything like this in Afghanistan; it is beautiful. Sunlight dances on the waves as we roar past. The helicopter lands in one of the few flat areas in this hilly region, and I disembark.

A soldier on a quad bike drives me over the dam to reach FOB Zeebrugge, the outpost for the British soldiers here. It is built on the side of a steep, rocky hill. Two smaller outposts, Sparrowhawk East and Sparrowhawk West, are placed at either side of the hill. I am told that the soldiers of the company—C Company, of the 3 Rifles Battalion—take turns to rotate up to Sparrowhawk positions. From there, they hold a commanding view of the surrounding lands, and can accurately engage Taliban forces from some distance away.

I arrive at Zeebrugge, and am given a brief about the area. Fairly strong Taliban presence, quite a few IEDs, and so on. Fairly standard for Helmand then. The big issue here is that the troops are relatively cut off from help—it's over fifty kilometres to the nearest British base, which is in Sangin.

There is an operation taking place tomorrow, in which the company will be pushing to the northern Forward Line of Enemy Troops—known as a 'FLET'. The C company commander, a major named Mike, agrees that I can accompany the soldiers.

SATURDAY 14 NOVEMBER

3.00 p.m.—I join the 3 RIFLES Fire Support Group (FSG) as they head out to secure some of the ground prior to the operation. These guys work in Jackal vehicles—four wheeled, open topped, and bristling with weaponry. We leave FOB Zeebrugge, and drive through the town of Tangye, which neighbours the dam. In previous years, the bazaar here would have been bustling with life. Now it's a ghost town.

Progress is slow, since vulnerable parts of the road and any suspicious-looking objects have to be thoroughly checked with metal detectors. I find myself nodding off in the back of the Jackal, the November sun providing comfortable warmth as we slowly inch forward. I much prefer Helmand in the winter.

9.00 p.m.—We spend the night on a hill overlooking the northern FLET. No sign of Taliban activity thus far. I will be spending the night here, then linking up with the soldiers who will be pushing into the FLET on foot

Beautiful but deadly; the district of Kajaki.

tomorrow. The FSG will remain here to provide covering fire should the ground troops run into any problems. It's a chilly night tonight; fortunately I remember warm clothing this time.

SUNDAY 15 NOVEMBER

5.00 a.m.—Wake up. Cold. Mornings like this present a unique dilemma—do I wear lots of warm clothing underneath my body armour and helmet, or do I dress ready for physical exertion and just patiently wait for the sun to become sufficiently warm? The danger of wearing too much warm clothing is that one can pretty much guarantee that combat, or some other pressing need, will render it nigh on impossible to strip off the helmet and body armour to remove the warm clothing, and thus the unfortunate person will have to sweat, sweat, and sweat. I decide to freeze for now, since I don't want to be running around later with a fleece on.

I am driven—quad bike again—to meet with the soldiers who will be advancing on foot today. I grab my bag, and fall into the line. The sun begins to peek over the mountains.

Like yesterday, progress is slow. Every inch of ground is swept by soldiers with metal detectors. Behind them, other men stoop and squirt talcum powder on the path, indicating to the column behind them the areas that are safe to tread in. In order to get good shots of the soldiers walking, I have to dart out of the line every now and then, but before I start to record, I make sure that my feet are firmly within the white powdered markings.

3.00 p.m.—We've been inching forward with our back-breaking loads for most of the day now. Sweating. I think I made the right clothing decision earlier. The soldiers clear compounds slowly, making sure that the Taliban haven't pushed in from their established FLET, which is drawing steadily closer. Checking compounds for bombs is a painstaking process, as the Taliban have been known to embed devices in walls and doorways—it suddenly becomes a case of three-dimensional detection, not just confined to the floor.

As we near the FLET, the Taliban begin to speak on their radios. They can see us coming, and are working out when and where to engage us. It's always a rather chilling feeling, knowing that invisible eyes are watching you walk, plotting your demise with every step.

The column arrives at the first Taliban-held compound. Unlike other places I have been in Helmand, the northern area of Kajaki is wide open, clear desert space with compounds spread out a good distance from each other. I highly doubt that any Taliban would have waited around in this compound for forty soldiers to walk slowly toward them. Despite that fact, we crouch alongside the southern edge of the large wall, as engineers prepare breaching charges to blast an entrance. Two soldiers throw grenades over the wall to wound or kill any Taliban who may have waited around against the odds. The wall charge detonates with a large concussion, covering everybody in dust, and the first troops charge through the new opening.

As suspected, it is empty. Everybody rests for a moment in the shade of the baked-mud walls. I begin to wonder whether the Taliban will bother fighting at all today. As I think this, an order comes through that there is a suspected Taliban bunker fifty meters north of our position, and that the soldiers are to clear it. Six men are chosen to go forward. I find myself volunteering to accompany them. I slightly annoy myself when I do this—I just feel that I have an inbuilt mechanism in my head 'not to be the one that is left behind'. It's completely open ground after the compound, so we will be sitting ducks if any Taliban do decide to fire at us. Insurgent radio chatter comes through: 'Shoot at the British if they leave the compound'. Deeply unwelcome news.

Jamie, a young corporal who is in charge of the six-man bunker clearance team, draws out our plan in the sand. It's quite a simple one—we will advance using metal detectors, and then the soldiers will cover each other as they check the suspected bunker. We step out into the open. I've rarely felt as exposed as I do now. Judging by the hunched, wincing soldiers around me, they feel the same. Step by step, we edge forward. Everything seems silent. My breathing seems deafening. Suddenly there is a distant gunshot. PIAAOWWW! A bullet whizzes over our heads. Sniper. 'Get down!' shouts Jamie. I throw myself to the ground, taking cover behind a woefully small gorse bush, which is about the size of my face. Jamie thinks that the shot came from a compound about eight hundred meters away.

The fact that the bullet didn't make a 'crack' sound means that it had sufficiently slowed down from where it was fired. The soldier beside me begins to return fire with his machine gun. Jamie runs forward and leaps into a wide trench system. The rest of us follow him, and begin to work our way toward the objective.

We finally reach the bunker, which turns out to be a mound of sandy earth, and return to the rest of the soldiers in the compound without incident. The post-combat euphoria sets in. Although it was a fairly short engagement, as firefights go, everybody is laughing and recounting the various emotions felt when the sniper took a potshot. I am glad that nobody got shot for the sake of a pile of dirt.

8.00 p.m.—We bed down for the night. Soldiers with night vision man the walls of the compound, seeing if they can catch any Taliban sneaking out to lay bombs for our departure tomorrow.

MONDAY 16 NOVEMBER

Uneventful night. We pack up and prepare to move back to FOB Zeebrugge. Sleeping on hard ground always makes me feel like I have been punched in the kidneys when I wake up; I will be glad to trade a fairly solid compound floor for a moderately comfortable military-issue camp bed tonight.

9.00 a.m.—We exit the compound and begin to trudge back. CRACKCRACKCRACK! A staccato burst of incoming fire from the Taliban snaps over our heads. It's coming from behind us. I turn and run as fast as I can to the back of the column. The FSG, who are still in their position on the hill, watching our extraction, begin to pour fire into the Taliban positions. From where we are, the soldiers here cannot see where the fire is coming from, and the order is given to continue the withdrawal.

We pass by the base of the hill, which the FSG are firing from. Keen to have more combat footage on tape than a single sniper shot, I ask Sam, the platoon commander, if I can run up to the FSG. In wonderful deference to the usual health and safety issues that constrict my movement, he agrees. I run up the hill as fast as I can—it's far steeper than I thought—and arrive at the FSG a panting wreck. Incoming fire is sporadic now; the astonishing weight of fire poured out by the Jackals has clearly subdued the Taliban's intentions for a clean parting shot. 'Air strike incoming!' a soldier near me yells, 'sixty seconds until impact!' While bombs are not the ideal way to end an engagement—due to the COIN strategy that is now in effect—there are no civilians at all in this area, and thus British troops operating here have more leeway when it comes to firepower. I sink to the ground to steady the camera on the doomed compound, glad to have a breather. The sound of an American B1 bomber can be heard getting steadily louder.

The compound erupts in a cloud of black smoke and fire. For a moment, the destruction unfolds in near-perfect silence, since the compound is several kilometres away, and a few seconds later the sound of the blast reaches us. This is the first time I have witnessed an air strike being used on Taliban fighters that have been shooting at the soldiers I am directly attached to. It's an odd feeling, seeing the black smoke curl upwards. On one hand, I almost feel sorry for them—the sheer violence of a bomb going off must be terrifying beyond all words, but on the other hand, they were attempting to kill us.

Drive back to Zeebrugge with the FSG.

TUESDAY 17 NOVEMBER

Spend the night on Sparrowhawk East. The difference in temperature here, despite the fact that it is only several hundred meters above Zeebrugge, is surprising. The view up here is incredible—I can now understand why the Taliban hate the fact that soldiers with long-ranged weapons can sit up here, nigh on invincible, and dominate the surrounding territory.

WEDNESDAY 18 NOVEMBER

Besides the British and Afghan soldiers, there are three other rather interesting residents in FOB Zeebrugge—a small band of incredibly diverse dogs. Legend has it that these dogs were here when the British took over the base, and they are lovingly passed on from unit to unit every time a rotation takes place. The soldiers have given them names. 'AK'—named after the rifle, I presume—is probably the biggest dog I have ever seen; he looks more like a polar bear, and spends most of the time sleeping outside the mess hall. 'Tangye'—named after the nearby village—is an athletic black Labrador. He is a favourite of many troops here; during firefights he runs up and down the line of soldiers, barking enthusiastically. One soldier tells me that in a recent IED strike, when body parts were scattered everywhere, Tangye—trying to assist his human friends—took it upon himself to pick up a leg and carry it to the medical helicopter. The final dog, given the curious name 'Gay Dog', looks like a small wolf.

FRIDAY 20 NOVEMBER

Another small operation, pushing into the southern FLET this time. Completely different terrain to the northern area. There is vegetation, and the familiarly claustrophobic compounds and alleyways. The infamous 611 road—which starts in Kajaki and runs down to Sangin—bisects this small town. It is so full of IEDs, however, that none of the soldiers bother to use it; several Afghan soldiers were killed two weeks ago when their vehicle hit a device here.

AK, the polar bear dog, saunters over to us—it seems that he will be gracing us with his presence on this operation. He is followed by the galloping Tangye, and the timid Gay Dog. Everybody's morale increases at the presence of the canines.

Due to the sheer amount of walls, shrubs, nooks, and crannies that could hide IEDs, every hundred meters that we move takes around an hour. The Royal Navy bomb disposal guys have their work cut out for them, having to investigate many suspected bombs. Several turn out to be the real thing, and we have to wait while they painstakingly detonate them.

A small surveillance plane—operated by some soldiers in Zeebrugge—crash lands near us, and we are told to look for it; it's undesirable that the Taliban get their hands on the technology, since they don't seem to understand its capabilities at the moment. 'We heard them talking about one of the little planes last week,' a soldier tells me, 'they were saying "the

British have even trained mice to fly small planes against us now!"' I wonder if the Taliban were being serious or not.

After several hours of sweaty searching, it is eventually found. Nobody quite wants to think about the risk involved in searching for the small plane—the Taliban have been fairly active on the radio, and bombs are everywhere—but, as one of the Navy guys tells me, it's all about perspective. 'Saying that we spent ages looking for a toy plane sounds bad,' he says, 'but if you say: "We spent hours risking our lives to rescue a downed aircraft", it sounds much better.' I think he has a point there.

SUNDAY 22 NOVEMBER

I am taken on a tour of the actual Kajaki dam itself by a pleasant South African security contractor named Benny. It is a fairly impressive construction, and I am able to get some good shots. I ask about the famous 'third turbine'. In 2008, there was a large operation to drive a huge turbine from Kandahar to Kajaki. The aim was that this third turbine would supplement the existing two, and help to provide power to both Kandahar and Helmand Provinces. The operation was a success, with hundreds of soldiers, troops, and aircraft playing a part in protecting the convoy from the Taliban. As I now ask if I can see the third turbine, Benny laughs ruefully. 'It's over there,' he says, pointing to a large tarpaulin covered object.

Benny explains that although the turbine reached Kajaki safely, the necessary electrical lines to relay the power out to Kandahar and Helmand are not in place; the existing lines are too weak, and would not be able to handle the megawatts that the dam would be putting out. The third turbine, therefore, sits here inertly, waiting for the power lines to be replaced. I ask Benny if he has any idea when work is due to commence on this. 'Not anytime soon, bru,' he says wistfully.

TUESDAY 24 NOVEMBER

6.00 p.m.—Flying to Sangin as the sun begins to set. Cold air rips through the helicopter as one of the RAF gunners slides open the side door; any who have tried to doze on this short flight are blasted into wakefulness. Soon we touch down in FOB Jackson—the primary ISAF base in the Sangin district. In the centre of Jackson sits a bullet riddled, crumbled building. When British paratroopers first arrived here in 2006, it was in that building that they held off repeated waves of Taliban attackers. Several men lost their lives during that summer, and British losses here have risen steadily since; many claim that it is the single most deadly place in all of Helmand. A 3 RIFLES soldier was killed here last week, victim of a Taliban sharpshooter.

Two snipers from the FSG who were in Kajaki with me also disembark from the helicopter—rumour has it that they are being brought in to help counter the Taliban sniper threat.

Emma, the 3 RIFLES press officer, welcomes me to Sangin and puts me in a tent with the snipers. Tomorrow night we will be departing to Patrol Base Blenheim, a small base that is currently being held by a platoon of British soldiers in conjunction with some Afghan troops. I ask Emma if there is much going on at Blenheim. 'They are under attack every day,' she says, 'are you definitely sure you are happy to go there?' I nod, it would feel wrong to shy away from the discomfort and terror of living at Blenheim when soldiers are experiencing it day in, day out.

WEDNESDAY 25 NOVEMBER

My home church in the UK has asked that I preach in December when I get back to the UK for Christmas leave—it's Mel and I who will be back for the festivities this year. I spend the day, sitting in my tent in FOB Jackson, writing a sermon about Mary, the mother of Jesus, and the visitation of the angel to her. It feels slightly odd to be preparing a sermon in one of the most dangerous places in the world, but I decide that focusing on it will stop me from worrying, or trying to imagine myself without any legs or arms.

7.00 p.m.—As darkness begins to fall in Sangin, I go for a walk around the camp, and listen to 'Amazing Grace' on my iPod. I thank God for keeping me safe thus far, and ask that he will continue to watch over me. Of all the times I have had to trust him in my life, none seem as pressing or immediate as imminent combat. So many people are injured or killed in Sangin, I have to stop for a moment and consider that there is a very real chance of being hurt or killed here. I ask God that whatever he has planned for me, that he gives me the ability to honour him through it—whether in perfect health, or grievous injury.

Walk back to the tent. The snipers are already asleep. We are departing in about seven hours, under the cover of darkness.

THURSDAY 26 NOVEMBER

2.00 a.m.—Arrive at the FOB Jackson vehicle staging area, and crawl into the back of a Mastiff– one of the most heavily armoured vehicles in the British arsenal—to depart from the FOB.

Inside the Mastiff we are packed once again like bleak tinned fish, draped on top of various bags and equipment. A rifle butt digs into my back. I am positioned near the front of the Mastiff, and I look on in fascination and terror as the driver slowly guides us through the streets of Sangin. The Mastiff is quite a new vehicle, and it is fitted with thermal equipment that enables the driver to navigate by looking at a large screen which displays the feed from the external camera. I watch the screen, mesmerized, wondering what it would feel like to have a bomb go off underneath us. So many vehicles have been hit in Sangin that I am basically expecting it to happen. Minutes pass, and we draw further away from FOB Jackson, through the bazaar, and into Blenheim.

We arrive without incident, the plan to move under the cover of night seeming to have paid off. It was a trouble-free trip; the Taliban radios didn't even spark to life. I grab my bag and, with the snipers, trudge up the small hill to PB Blenheim. It is too dark to make out much of the base, so I decide to have a proper look round when the sun comes up. We are shown to our camp beds, and gratefully collapse into slumber.

7.00 a.m.—Wake up. Look around. Blenheim—like all good combat outposts—is pretty spartan. It is ringed with Hesco barriers, and has small wooden guard towers—sangars—at each corner. The toilets are thick pipes hammered into the ground. Two large metal shipping containers sit in the centre of the base, with large camouflage tarpaulin sheets strung from either side, covering two rows of camp beds—the platoon's sleeping area.

The soldiers themselves cluster around a small fire, dusty, hard-eyed, and lean. H, the platoon sergeant, prods at some sizzling bacon and beans, and begins to dole it out, for all the world like a mother hen, to his men. Initially, they are all fairly standoffish with me. They have become very tightly-knit, bonded together by shared combat experience and isolation, but begin to soften when I rattle through my time served in Afghanistan, and previous military experience.

Kieran, an excitable corporal, comes over to introduce himself. He tells me about the fighting that has taken place here over the last few weeks. One of their guys was shot, he explains, as he was standing doing guard duty in one of the wooden sangars. The bullet struck him in the shoulder, and apparently he was smiling as they carried him to the medical helicopter. Flesh wounds like that are often viewed as a golden ticket out of combat—they are rarely life changing, but give a 'cool scar' and a war story to tell the grandchildren. The fact that the sniper was able to hit the soldier from so far away, however, is a rather worrying thought—whoever he is, he seems to be far more skilled than the average 'spray and pray' Taliban who often fire their weapons without aiming properly.

The plan to get the sniper who, according to Taliban radio chatter, is named 'Gulab', involves sending out a patrol several times per day, hoping to lure him out so the British snipers can kill him. It's going to be quiet for the next few days though, because Eid Al-Mubarak, an Islamic special day—'the Afghan Christmas', a solider tells me—is happening tomorrow, and the Taliban are likely to start fighting a day or so after that.

FRIDAY 27 NOVEMBER

I wish a happy Eid to the Afghan soldiers on our base, who are sitting around eating mutton. They reply with happy grunts, flashing toothy smiles at me.

I sit around with the British guys. There isn't too much to do here. Some soldiers play chess, some work out with makeshift equipment, others read a book, and some just sit and talk. Carlos, a South African rifleman, who is older than any of the other riflemen, is gently teased for the wisdom that he dishes out to his colleagues, grinning at the 'young pups' around him. Brett, an Australian—like Carlos, a non-British person serving in the British Army—lends me a science fiction book. Like me, he enjoys so-called 'geeky' things.

Kieran shows me a journal that he is writing for his wife back home. He got married fairly closely to his deployment, and is caught up in the starry-eyed romance of the newlywed. He has faithfully been recording his experiences—day by day—since he arrived here. Each entry contains a few sentences about how much he misses and loves his wife; I hope that he survives to give it to her in person.

SATURDAY 28 NOVEMBER

Patrol into the neighbouring village today. The soldiers wish the locals happy Eid. Everywhere we go, we are greeted with blank, unfriendly stares—of all the places I have been to, Sangin definitely seems to be the most hostile. As ever, movement is slow (the IED threat, as I can't stress enough, is ridiculously high here) and I decide not to step out to the right or the left to get a shot of the patrol. It's not worth risking my legs for. The Taliban talk to each other over their walkie-talkies—they can see us walking, but are deciding whether to engage us or not. I wonder if Gulab is watching us—is he taking aim right now?

Make it back to base without incident. Phew.

SUNDAY 29 NOVEMBER

Sitting on my camp bed reading my Bible. CRACK CRACK! Two shots ring out; the bullets flying right over Blenheim. People cheer ironically—the Taliban are announcing their return from the Eid break.

5.00 p.m.—There are several more shots fired today, but they seem rather half-hearted efforts as opposed to sustained attacks. Kieran offers me his British camouflage trousers to wear on patrols. Cameramen in this area have been coming under specific attack, the Taliban logic being that a video making them look bad is probably more damaging to their cause than a single soldier. A British combat camera guy recently told me that he heard the Taliban saying 'shoot the cameraman first' over their radios. If I wear Kieran's spare trousers, then hopefully I will not stand out like a sore thumb when the Taliban are picking their targets. Hopefully.

MONDAY 30 NOVEMBER

On patrol today with Corporal Ricky's section. Ricky is a lively guy—about my age, with a slight accent, hailing from north-west of London. He has grown a rather impressive handlebar moustache for the deployment, and has a reputation for disregarding his own safety to look after the men under his command.

As we walk through a boggy field—bombs are less likely to be in the middle of a field than they are on a well-used route like a path or road—the Taliban begin to talk about 'how they can see the British in a field', and they give the order to open fire on us. It is a very unsettling experience: we are headed back to Blenheim, and our backs are facing the place they are likely to fire from if they do engage us. The hairs on the back of my neck rise in anticipation. Once again, the horrible feeling of knowing you are being watched, probably through a rifle scope, and that your life could be ended at any second.

We make it out of the field without incident—much to everyone's relief—and we walk up an alleyway toward the base. Ricky turns to me, knowing full well that I am here to try and get combat footage. 'Unlucky, Josh mate. Maybe next ti-' CRACKCRACKCRACK! Before Ricky can finish his sentence, the Taliban finally open fire, the bullets slapping into the top of the mud wall to our right. Why they chose to do so when we are in an alleyway—and therefore able to take cover—when they could have fired when we were in the open field, I have no idea. But as I gratefully crawl over to a thick mud wall to hide, it doesn't seem to matter that much. Everybody is laughing—it was like a moment of slapstick comedy, with Ricky being proved wrong with almost disastrous consequences.

Richard, the rifleman to my left, returns fire with his light machine gun.

CRACK! The incoming shot seems less accurate, wilder than the opening salvo. The snipers back in Blenheim also begin to engage the compound that the Taliban are firing from; the insurgents soon fall silent. We patrol back to Blenheim, unharassed.

TUESDAY 1 DECEMBER

The compound that the Taliban were firing from is perched on a small hill about 500 metres away from Blenheim and at roughly the same height. It is called Compound 86. The ground between us drops in height—like the snipers in Blenheim, the Taliban in Compound 86 have a commanding view of the surrounding terrain.

One of the snipers explains to me how the Taliban fire. They make a small hole in the compound wall, and then fill it with a brick. When it is time to fire at the British, they remove the brick, stick their muzzles through, and open fire. Holes like this are called 'murder holes', and they grant good protection to the Taliban, as anybody shooting at them would

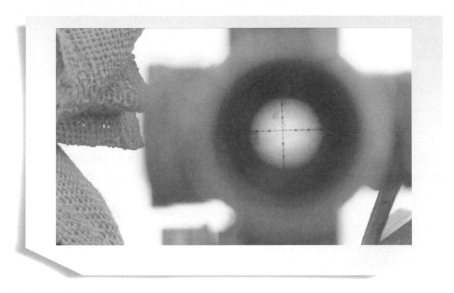

The view of a murder hole through a sniper's scope.

have to hit inside the hole—which is smaller than a football—from several hundred meters away. It's an effective way for the enemy to fight, and they have pre-made murder holes all over the area, giving them a variety of positions to fire at us from. During patrols, the soldiers carry a can of yellow spray paint that they use to paint a ring around any murder holes that they find—making them easier to spot from Blenheim if the Taliban use them.

11.00 a.m.—We patrol up the 611, which runs directly past Blenheim, and approach Compound 86. Heart thumping. We are hoping to lure out the sniper. Feel like a worm dangling on the end of a fishing hook—I expect the other guys do too. One hundred meters before we reach Compound 86, we swing round—in a hook-shaped formation, I think to myself ironically. Curving round in this formation means that every single person, as they reach the apex of the bend, is the single closest man to the enemy position. Every muscle tenses. I bite my lip; my body feels like it does when expecting a blow. Taliban chatter away on their radios. I clear the apex; relieved not to be the nearest man anymore. CRACKCRACKCRACK! It was to be expected really, there's no way that these fish would pass up such bait. In conventional warfare, the soldiers would throw themselves off the road— which offers no protection—and into the nearest cover possible. In Sangin, though, doing that could mean running into a bomb that the Taliban plant in a position where they think a soldier might go to hide.

CRACK! CRACK! I sink to the ground, hoping that my diminished profile will make me less of a target. The soldiers around me begin to return fire. Dust kicks up around the Compound 86 murder hole as the bullets find their mark. As with other engagements, the Taliban fire ceases almost immediately, and we are left to trudge back to base, the adrenaline comedown leaving shaky limbs and tired expressions.

9.00 p.m.—Standing in the darkness, practicing a run through of my now-completed sermon. It seems bizarre to be doing this right now, but it feels like my slice of normality and comfort in the middle of this completely alien, dangerous place. I am stunned by the bravery of the soldiers here— walking out to be shot at, day in, day out, requires a special type of physical and mental strength. I am feeling the effects already; the fear, the worry, the hopelessness are beginning to gnaw at me after a week, and I can only imagine how the guys here—Ricky, Kieran, Brett, Carlos, Richard, and the others—will feel after six months in the district.

An Apache buzzes above me, silhouetted in the moonlight, keeping vigil as Sangin sleeps. The sense of comfort that the presence of this helicopter brings is palpable. As I watch it fly, I realize that it's quite similar to the idea of faith. When an Apache is present, you trust that it will keep you safe, trust that your chances of surviving increase dramatically. That's the level of faith that the heroes in the Old Testament—Moses, Joshua, and David to name a few—had in their God. In battle, he was their confidence and assurance, he was the one they trusted to protect them—and he didn't need to refuel. I thank him for giving me the courage to go out on patrol every day thus far, and ask that he teaches me to trust him like the old heroes did.

WEDNESDAY 2 DECEMBER

11.00 a.m.—On patrol, filming the soldiers spraying a new murder hole that has been found. After the hole has been marked—and substantially enlarged by a soldier with a pickaxe—we walk back to Blenheim. As we climb up the hill, the Taliban seize the chance to attack. CRACKCRACKCRACK! The opening three-shot burst has become a familiar beginning to firefights initiated here. We are caught out in the open, strung out on the dusty hill for all to see. CRACK! CRACK! The Taliban begin to fire again, they seem more determined than previous engagements.

The soldiers around me, lying flat on their stomachs, are not keen to randomly fire at will—a sea of compounds and rooftops lie before us, and firing at random could cause serious civilian casualties—and therefore the Taliban are free to fire with impunity for the moment. CRACKCRACKCRACK! That was close. I sit helplessly on my bottom, filming everything I can. CRACK! WHIZZ! Kieran suddenly spots where they are firing from 'Compound 86, gents! Fire! Fire!' Suspecting Compound 86 as the guilty party, most people are already aiming at it.

The desperate scramble over the sandbag walls of PB Blenhiem.

Grenades, machine gun fire, and sniper rifles open up against 86 in a deafening crescendo of violence. The Taliban fire wavers, but continues.

Being stuck in the open like this is not good, and Kieran orders that we begin to extract back into Blenheim. The problem is that this specific entrance to the base requires climbing up a ladder and rolling over a sandbag wall. We are going to have to go over one by one while everybody else fires at the Taliban. Kieran throws a purple smoke grenade to obscure our escape. CRACK! CRACK! They cannot see us specifically, but they are aiming at the purple smoke. Soldiers clamber up the ladder, and the other guys who were left in Blenheim reach out and haul their friends over the sandbags. My turn to go. Making the decision to stand up under fire is never an easy one. Reluctantly climb to my feet and sprint toward the ladder. CRACKCRACKCRACK! Incoming fire. BANG! BANG! Outgoing fire. At the ladder now, moving so fast that I don't even feel like I am climbing—I just throw myself upwards, into the welcoming grip of several gloved hands that pull me over the wall. Ricky cheers at me as I fall in an unceremonious heap 'There you go, Josh mate, finally got some good action, eh?'

I run over to where the snipers are shooting at Compound 86. BANG! 'Got him!' one of the snipers yells. Taliban fire ceases immediately. The sniper explains to me that he was watching a known murder hole, when he saw a hand reach out and remove a brick. A second later, a muzzle appeared in the hole. The sniper sent one shot through the hole— displaying remarkable accuracy from over five hundred meters—and the incoming fire stopped immediately. Was that Gulab? Is he dead?

Resolve to ask Danielle out for a coffee if I get through my time down here; it gives me a bit of hope to cling onto.

5.00 p.m.—The evening call to prayer sounds different tonight. The wailing voice is higher, younger. 'I think that means that at least one of the Taliban died today,' the sniper tells me. 'When somebody is killed, the Mullah—who usually sings the call to prayer—goes to administer the Muslim equivalent of the last rites, and it's the job of his eldest son to do the call to prayer instead.'

I show the footage of the firefight to the guys, who cheer and laugh as they see each other in action. Anybody who struggled to negotiate the ladder becomes the target of merciless teasing.

THURSDAY 3 DECEMBER

Another patrol, another brief skirmish. I think I have pulled my neck muscle—it fiercely jerks my head down every time I hear the dreaded 'crack!'

FRIDAY 4 DECEMBER

My final patrol with the guys today. Despite the stark and nerve-wracking nature of life here in Sangin, I will really miss the camaraderie and excitement of Blenheim.

We patrol north of the base, into a flat area of desert between compounds. Taliban radio chatter intensifies. Everybody is scanning the alleyways, windows, and doorways of the nearby compounds—Taliban could pop out and fire at any second.

We conduct a fishhook turn again (I absolutely loathe that moment when I am closest to the suspected enemy location!) and begin to walk back to base. Some would question the point of patrols like this—going for a walk—but it's important for the soldiers here to create a buffer zone of patrolling around Blenheim to stop the insurgents having free run of the area.

As we walk back, wishing we had eyes in the backs of our heads, there is a shout. I whip round, and time seems to slow down. Two Taliban have appeared out of an alleyway—astonishingly, the first I have seen in twenty months here. One is aiming a rocket-propelled grenade (RPG) launcher at us. In that awful split second, when we realize that there is no way that any of us can react quick enough to stop him firing at us, I begin to think that my number might be up. There is a loud 'BANG!' and the RPG Taliban keels forward as he fires. His RPG hits the ground several meters in front of him, exploding harmlessly as he falls to the ground, dead. I look back at Blenheim, and see the shape of one of the snipers—almost camouflaged beyond recognition—looking through a scope. He was the only person who was quick enough to react to stop the insurgent firing at us. He could well have saved somebody's life. The other Taliban fighter is long gone.

An hour later, once more, the high-pitched wail of the Mullah's son pierces the Sangin dusk.

SATURDAY 5 DECEMBER

A convoy arrives at Blenheim to bring supplies and ferry me back to FOB Jackson. I say goodbye to the guys here—it has been a genuine pleasure to be with them, and to share their lives and experiences for a week or so. We exchange email addresses, and I promise to email my footage to their loved ones.

In one of those 'once in an Afghan experience' strokes of blessing, I am able to get from Blenheim to Jackson to Bastion to Kabul in one day. Will picks me up from the airport. While I was away, we have had to move to HQ ISAF which, in many ways, is a good thing—we will be more 'plugged in' to what happens at HQ. Will very kindly packed up my half of the room, and ferried it over to HQ, a long and monotonous task. He really is a great guy. It's good to be back with the team.

Go to sleep, dreaming of Taliban snipers shooting at me.

11 Love

6 December 2009—31 January 2010

SUNDAY 6 DECEMBER

It's weird waking up at HQ, I think we will all miss the relative freedom and open spaces of Kabul Airbase; people and living spaces are packed in closely together here. I also suspect that there will be a fair amount of added bureaucracy here. I decide not to worry about this for now—my aim is to get my Kajaki and Sangin stories edited and uploaded before my leave next week.

Our new office is quite nice—it certainly beats working in my bedroom, like I did back in KAIA. In addition to the chairs, desks, and whiteboards, it seems that we have also inherited a cat, who a Dutch photographer has named 'George', and who seems to spend most of his life sleeping or mewing for food. Cats really do have an easy ride in life.

FRIDAY 11 DECEMBER

Thomas offers me a new contract, which would take me through to 2011. I think for a moment, and talk to Will, who is down in Kandahar. We both think that we can push one more year—disillusionment with everything here is slowly beginning to creep in, but I think that I can stave off its ravishing effects for another twelve months.

WEDNESDAY 16 DECEMBER

All stories are completed, flying home for several weeks tomorrow. I spend most of the night packing. Notice that Danielle is on Facebook chat. We talk for three hours, which I deem to be a good sign. Ask her for coffee next Tuesday. She agrees. Nervous.

SATURDAY 19 DECEMBER

Back in the UK. I've spent so long in Afghanistan now that being back home feels stranger than being away. My brother, who I haven't seen for two years, is back from the USA—where he lives—for Christmas. It's good to see him again.

10.00 a.m.—The church is doing carol singing on the local estate. I pop down to show my face and say hello to everyone. Danielle's mum and dad are there. I am slightly disappointed that she isn't.

SUNDAY 20 DECEMBER

See Danielle at church. She looks amazing—why does our coffee on Tuesday seem so far away?

TUESDAY 22 DECEMBER

Walking to Danielle's house. Pray as I walk. I ask God that above all other things—especially my desires—his will is done, and that he is honoured. It's challenging to do that, and instantly I start to get nagging little thoughts. 'What if you really like her, but God shows you that she isn't the one for you?' Try to ignore them. True obedience to God is laying everything at his feet and trusting in him—not treating him like a vending machine that I go to only when I want something.

Arrive at Danielle's place and ring the doorbell. She answers, and my heart immediately starts hammering. We walk to a nearby coffee shop, asking questions about each other.

Danielle explains further about the baby situation—she, like me, was backslidden, and engaged in an improper relationship. Despite warnings from her parents, and the nagging of her conscience, she fell pregnant. Despite the world seemingly crashing down around her, God used the pain to bring her back to him. Against the advice of her friends, she wanted to keep it. She also ended the relationship—the father was showing little interest in the baby—and moved back in with her parents, who had just moved down here to begin at my church. Now, being in a new place, without any friends, facing an uncertain time as a single mother, Danielle's faith in God was being put to the test. She was determined to honour him in this, despite the difficulties that her mistakes had caused.

We speak for several hours; neither of us want it to end. Seeing the waitresses looking slightly impatient at our lengthy stay, I ask Danielle if she would like to go to the cinema? Yes, she would!

After the film, I ask her if she would like to go for dinner, and the 'coffee' finally turns into an all-day date. As we talk, I begin to feel the first flutter in my heart, mixed with trepidation. I am falling for this girl, and I have just signed a contract to be in a war zone for another year. This could get grim. Try to ignore it—there are still a couple of weeks to play with before I have to return.

1.00 a.m.—I drop Danielle home. Being six months pregnant, I have probably already kept her out longer than is entirely sensible. I ask her if she would mind if we did Bible studies together over the next few weeks. She answers that she would love to. We embrace and part ways. I feel like singing, dancing, and shouting with sheer exhilaration. Too excited to even think about sleeping, I go for a walk with two of my dearest old school friends, Fred and Trevor, around some of our old haunts. 'Gentlemen,' I say. 'I don't want to speak too soon, but I think that I might be in love.'

As I lie in bed that night, thanking God that the date went so well, I realize that if we do fall in love, and start seeing each other, it's going to be difficult with a new baby on the way. Would I be prepared to potentially be the father? An odd thought. In years past, I could barely look after a hamster, but now, potentially a baby boy? Probably too early to be thinking about that, Josh.

WEDNESDAY 23 DECEMBER

I am told about an Afghan Christian named Fahran, who fled the country due to persecution. He is about to be deported back there. Must be terrifying. I resolve to see if I can make contact with him while he is out there.

On the train with Dad, I talk about Danielle. He chuckles. 'Josh, you are aware that when a Christian man asks a girl to do Bible studies with him, that it is an indication that he is potentially interested in marrying her? Be careful, son—don't go breaking any hearts!' A good point. In the midst of my feelings, I must try to be responsible.

THURSDAY 24 DECEMBER

Christmas Eve. Bible study with Danielle. We have a really enjoyable time together, looking at God's Word and praying. There's something incredible about taking the thing that means so much to you personally, and sharing it with someone else. I have definitely fallen for this girl, and have thus boarded an emotional rollercoaster that will take an inescapable sharp plunge downwards on 6 January.

FRIDAY 25 DECEMBER

Spend an enjoyable Christmas Day with the family—it's good to be home with them at this time of year. Irritated at my hopelessly impractical emotions, that make me rueful that I cannot see Danielle today.

SATURDAY 26 DECEMBER

Go for a night-time walk in the snowy woods with Danielle. I have decided that I am going to tell her that I like her. Despite all indications pointing at the fact that she probably likes me too, I am absolutely terrified. In past relationships, I have been rather cowardly, and often handled the critical 'I really like you' moment by text, so as to save my blushes if I am spurned. I have decided that it probably isn't very responsible to do it this time round.

We find a bench and sit down. I will my mouth to form the words that will begin my expression of interest, inwardly furious it when it stubbornly refuses. Why is this so hard? Over the last twelve months, I have helped to save a wounded soldier under fire, I have been shot at numerous times, I have been sniper bait, but the idea of telling a girl that I like her seems, at this moment, to be the singularly most terrifying thing I have ever done. I finally master myself and get the words out—albeit rather clumsily.

Danielle is slightly shocked, she really likes me too—thank goodness—but she thought that I would never ask, that I was just meeting up with her because I felt sorry for her or something. That, fortunately, isn't the case. We walk back through the moonlit trees. My heart is singing. That's confirmed. The 6th January, the day of my flight back to Afghanistan, is going to hurt a lot.

THURSDAY 31 DECEMBER

Go up to London with Danielle to watch New Year's Eve firework display. My departure date is growing inexorably closer, and we are trying to make the most of the time we have.

We hold hands and cuddle as the clock strikes midnight, but while everyone around us is kissing, we decide to hold off. Having made mistakes in the past, rushing into the physical aspect of relationships, we want to focus on the actual compatibility of us as people before we take anything else further. After my grim stint of girl-chasing in 2008, I have also decided that the next girl I kiss will be the one I want to marry, nobody else.

It's an impressive firework show, but is soon eclipsed by the thousands of people trying to get home on a sporadic train service. Trying to get a heavily pregnant girl through a massive crowd—all shuffling like tired zombies—and home safely proves to be an exhausting experience. Finally drop her off in the early hours of New Years' Day. Return home and collapse into bed, comatose.

MONDAY 4 JANUARY

Two days to go until departure. This is going to be absolutely brutal.

TUESDAY 5 JANUARY

Take Danielle out for a final date. In a pleasing bit of symmetry, we mirror our first date by doing an all-day coffee/cinema/meal thing. This is very likely to be our last date as we know it—her baby is due in March, and it is unlikely that I will be home from Afghanistan until April at the very least. Things are going to change so much, I am absolutely terrified. Will she still like me after the baby comes? What if she falls for somebody else while I am away? What if I am hurt or killed?

I try to ignore these feelings and enjoy the evening. Not very successful, if I'm honest. Like trying to tidy a room around a hulking elephant with baleful red eyes. With every smile, laugh, or romantic word exchanged, I feel that there is something vast and horrible hanging over my head. Indeed, in conversation with Fred that night—who is currently enduring a transatlantic relationship with the woman who will later become his wife—this feeling that we both know too well is formally codified as 'the elephant'.

WEDNESDAY 6 JANUARY

6.00 a.m.—Mum and Dad—who are along for moral support—take me to the airport. On the way, we stop and pick up Danielle who wants to come and say goodbye. I didn't sleep much last night; my heart feels like it is torn in two. Nobody says much as we drive toward the airport, the elephant is crushing any joy or meaningful conversation out of existence.

We arrive, this is it. How am I going to do this? Tears spring to my eyes; I haven't cried in public since I was a child. Danielle and I, choking through the sobs, tell each other how much we will miss each other. We are holding saying off 'I love you' until we are sure, although it seems to be the unspoken sentiment hanging in the air. I am a snotty, tearful wreck. We cling onto each other and say a prayer, and then goodbye. Mum is in tears. This is an absolute emotional train-wreck; I just want to curl up in a ball and die. I wouldn't wish pain like this on anyone. We part. I watch as mum gently leads the sobbing Danielle away. She turns to look at me once more, an image that is seared into my consciousness, and then, in an instant, they are gone.

I instantly retreat to the nearest toilet cubicle in an attempt to compose myself. 'Jesus, Jesus, Jesus,' I pray to myself, like I said in my first firefight back in March last year, simply unable to articulate anything else. How on earth can I get through another year like this? I feel like my heart has been crushed. Text from my Dad. 'Love you son. Take this pain, and use it to imagine the pain of separation that God felt when Jesus hung on the cross. Honour him in this time. Love you. Fath'. Tears flow even harder—there's something about the love of my Dad that does that to me. And, of course, he is right. That moment when Jesus took the sins of the world upon him and God, his Father, turned his face away from his only Son was a heartbreaking moment for both of them, borne out of love for the human race.

I am finally able to leave the toilet. I text Danielle, reiterating everything that was said through the sobs. Check-in and boarding. As we take off—feeling like I am leaving my insides trailing behind like streamers—I begin to think about what is ahead. The Josh of 2009 seems like another person. During the various combat missions of last year, I thought of myself as a fairly faith-filled person. After all, I did what I had to do, and was able to do it without becoming a fearful wreck. Now, the thought of getting shot at, the thought of being in combat when I have something to lose is truly frightening. Lord, I have nothing left, no strength, no resources, no will. I need you to get me through this, and I need your grace to help me honour you in this situation, a situation I really don't want to be in any more.

5.00 p.m.—Land in Copenhagen. Due to the heavy snow here—the presence of snow bringing a pang to my heart as I think of the snowy days I spent with Danielle—I stay with the night with David and his girlfriend Laura. David now lives in Copenhagen after finishing in Afghanistan early last year, and is now doing European-based NATO work from here. I dimly remember mentally looking down on him last year for leaving the war for the sake of a relationship. Being in a relationship has completely transformed my thinking—I can't believe that he was even able to do a whole year.

David and Laura do their best to reassure me—they are two of the few people who know what Danielle and I will be going through for the next year.

THURSDAY 7 JANUARY

At Copenhagen Airport with Danish soldiers. Watch their goodbyes with loved ones, glad that I don't have to go through that again today. I think that I have developed an irrational fear of farewells now.

FRIDAY 8 JANUARY

Back in Kabul, with my 'second family'. Ruth is also suffering heartache issues—it's always oddly comforting to know somebody else that is suffering with you. Will and I are invited to play football with some French soldiers tonight, usually something that I enjoy doing, but I just feel completely empty. I seriously begin to worry about the next year—I really don't see how I can do this. A major problem I face in life is that I get overly attached to things and, as David often observes laughingly, 'I don't do things by halves'.

10.00 p.m.—Speak to Danielle on Skype. The Internet connection is infuriating, but I cannot complain, the guys back at PB Blenheim in Sangin don't have any sort of connection to the outside world.

Danielle and I decide that the verse we are going to memorize and have as 'our verse' during this difficult time is from 2 Corinthians 4. It reads:

'All this is for your benefit, so that the grace that is reaching more and more people may cause thanksgiving to overflow to the glory of God. Therefore we do not lose heart. Though outwardly we are wasting away, yet inwardly we are being renewed day by day. For our light and momentary troubles are achieving for us an eternal glory that far outweighs them all.' (2 Corinthians 4:15–17)

TUESDAY 12 JANUARY

I appear to have somewhat shot myself in the foot. Because the British and Americans in Helmand are so pleased with the footage I got last year, they have invited me down for another 'thing'—I suspect another big operation—in February. My desire for adventure and combat is at its lowest ebb, but at the end of the day this is my job; I just have to go with it.

THURSDAY 14 JANUARY

Every day we receive a report that details all the incidents that have happened throughout Afghanistan that day. As a habit, I always check the places that I have visited—particularly Kajaki and Sangin—seeing if anybody I know might have been hurt. The times that I have seen Blenheim mentioned thus far have been ineffectual IED attacks, or firefights, neither with casualties. Today's report reads differently:

IED ATTACK: 13 JAN 10, east of PB BLENHEIM, SANGIN District, HELMAND PROVINCE: An IED targeted an ISAF patrol, resulting in one (UK) ISAF WIA.

Oh no. An IED strike near Blenheim, one ISAF soldier—obviously British—wounded in action. Who is it? I think of the guys that I met in December: Brett, Kieran, Ricky, Carlos, and the others. Has one of them been injured? I email my various contacts, asking if anyone has heard the identity of the injured person. No reply yet.

FRIDAY 15 JANUARY

It's Ricky. He is in a serious condition—he has lost both legs and parts of his hand, as well as an eye, and has severe shrapnel damage all over his body. He is on the way back to the UK for emergency treatment at the moment. It's absolutely shocking news. I think back to the way that he would joke around, the way that he actually cared about me getting the footage I needed. And now, if he survives, he faces the rest of his life with these horrific injuries.

Praying for him seems to be a woefully inadequate response, but it's all that I can do. I also pray for the rest of the guys at Blenheim—it must be awful for them.

MONDAY 18 JANUARY

In the east with US soldiers for a few days. It's been a while since I went to this part of Afghanistan, having spent most of my 2009 embeds in Helmand. Phone signal still works out here, thankfully, and I am able to text Danielle sporadically.

TUESDAY 19 JANUARY

Going out to a humanitarian aid drop, run by the Afghan army, in a local town. As I board the US vehicle, a soldier says to me: 'Don't be scared, reporter. We should be OK if we come under attack.' I bite back an acidic response. I really hate it when soldiers are condescending—which doesn't actually happen much at all, thankfully. The fact that it has come from a soldier who has only been in Afghanistan for two months, who has not been in any serious firefights, during a period when I am finding life so tough almost causes me to snap. But I decide to ignore it; it's easy to have a good attitude when things are going right for me, but a whole different story when the chips are down—it's times like this when honouring God in my thoughts, words, and actions are critical.

SUNDAY 24 JANUARY

Back in Kabul. Preaching my first sermon in the chapel at HQ today. Unlike the KAIA chapel, there is a chaplain here, and a fairly large congregation. Keen to continue preaching, I asked the chaplain, Bill, if I could have a sermon slot every now and then. After listening to mp3s of my previous attempts, and looking at my notes (making sure that I am not a heretic, no doubt!), he kindly agreed.

I preach from James 1, the passage that explains why we should consider it a joy when we are faced with trials and difficulties in life. I feel that it is somehow rather appropriate to the situation I am faced with at the moment, and as I preach, I speak for my own benefit as much as anyone else's. Trials help Christians to test their faith, which in turn produces the perseverance that leads to maturity.

As I preach, I understand why God has let this pain happen—he is doing this because he wants to make me a better Christian. He has raised the bar to a whole new level so that I have to completely and utterly trust in him, even when it hurts to do so. My faith in firefights last year was real, but it was all so exciting that it was very easy to trust in God. Now that I am struggling, and having an emotionally rotten time, it has suddenly become much, much harder to do.

WEDNESDAY 27 JANUARY

E-mail from the deported Afghan Christian, Fahran, who has recently returned to Kabul. He is asking for my mobile number so that we can try to meet at some stage soon. He explains that it is not easy for him to be in public, and therefore meeting up might prove to be difficult. I offer to pick him up in our car, then drive somewhere that he will feel at ease. No reply, although I imagine that getting on the Internet is pretty hard for him.

SUNDAY 31 JANUARY

Flying down to Helmand tomorrow for the 'thing'. I have been told to plan to stay down there for up to three weeks. I don't imagine that it is going to be easy to speak to Danielle while I am down there, and therefore we try to make the most of our final Skype call tonight. I am doing my best to put on a brave face, saying that everything will be OK, but privately I have my own misgivings. What if we are to become one of those tragic stories of love cut off before it could properly blossom? There have been many people throughout the years who have trusted in God, and have met bad ends—faith doesn't guarantee any happy endings in this life. Sure, there is heaven, but with such an immediate desire in my heart—to be with Danielle—I feel that if I die here, I will have missed out. I know in my heart that it isn't the right attitude to have, which I think is why God is allowing me to go through this, to show me that he should be the primary source of my comfort, security, and joy. It's tough.

What makes it worse is that Danielle's ex, who has got wind of the fact that she is in a relationship, has now appeared in the picture claiming that he wants to be part of the baby's life (after not showing any interest thus far), and even making an attempt to try and win her back. I take this news like a dagger in the heart. I hate that I am stuck here away from her. I hate that he is trying to get her back. How am I supposed to show love towards him, as Jesus commands us to, when every part of me screams cold hatred toward him? I always assumed that I was good at 'loving my enemies', because I didn't hate the Taliban for shooting at me. Once again, I am proved to be woefully short of what I believe about myself.

We say goodbye on Skype—she sheds tears, I struggle to contain my own—and end the call. I need to get my game face on, it's Helmand time.

12 Breaking Point

1 February 2010—24 March 2010

MONDAY 1 FEBRUARY

Fly down to Helmand. Lots of Afghan soldiers on the flight—I have a feeling that they are going to be featuring quite prominently in the 'thing'. Arrive at Bastion. The British have decided that I will be accompanying the Estonians for this operation, which I am thrilled about; I hold them in a special place within my heart after breaking my combat duck with them last March, almost a year ago. It's a different group of men, but I am told that there might still be one or two familiar faces around.

As I sit in the Estonian NSE, I notice one or two of them glancing over at me from their throng. Oh no, am I getting journalist-hate even now? One of them walks up to me. 'Aren't you the guy that did the videos with EstCoy 7?' he asks. EstCoy 7 was the team I was with last year. I answer yes. 'Ah, nice work man. Everybody in Estonia has seen those videos—we all have them on our laptops!' Brilliant—credentials are sorted, no journo-loathing here, then.

The new company commander, Mikhail, briefs me about the upcoming operation, which is happening in just under two weeks. It is called 'Operation Moshtarak'—which translates as 'together'. It is hoped that ISAF and Afghan forces, shoulder by shoulder, will demonstrate the increased capability of the Afghans to secure their land by conducting the largest joint operation of the conflict thus far. Like Operation Khanjar last summer with the US Marines, a large air assault will be taking place, dropping us into Nadi-Ali—the district where the fighting last March with EstCoy 7 occurred. The ISAF and Afghan forces will be clearing out the

Taliban and building new bases and checkpoints for the soldiers to man, in a bid to expand General McChrystal's COIN security bubble.

In the meantime, I will be heading down to FOB Wahid, the Estonian base on the edge of Nadi-Ali, to spend some time with the troops there before the operation launches.

WEDNESDAY 3 FEBRUARY

Estonian convoy down to Wahid. As we trundle along, passengers bouncing up and down in the back, I notice that even my thoughts about IEDs have changed. Before, I thought that if one did go off, it wouldn't seriously hurt me. Now, in this windowless, large metal coffin, I stare at the floor nervously, expecting it to suddenly be peeled away in a gigantic blast of shrapnel, heat, and dust. This change in my thinking is a remarkably unmanning experience. I think about H, the platoon sergeant in Blenheim, the married father of two young children, and the fear in his eyes before stepping out on patrol. Back then, I didn't understand it. Now I do. Having something precious to lose while in a combat zone is not a pleasant experience.

We reach Wahid safely, and I am put in a tent with a Finnish journalist named Niklas and several other Estonian soldiers. The next week or so here will involve a few low level patrols and rehearsals for the operation itself. Wahid—like every other small FOB here—is a ring of Hesco blocks with living quarters in the middle. It is bordered by a river, and therefore one part of the base is raised on a steep bank. The ground is cold and boggy, as January and February are rarely pleasant months to be in Helmand, with terrain often resembling World War One battlefields as opposed to a desert. I seem to be in the perfect vortex of despair right now—inwardly and outwardly.

THURSDAY 4 FEBRUARY

No patrols going out today. I am left with my own thoughts for the day; most of the Estonians only speak halting English, and therefore little is exchanged beyond a few pleasantries. I take to sitting on the raised bank, reading my Bible and praying. The grim thought I had on the eve of my departure—that faith in God does not necessarily mean that I will be with Danielle—begins to echo in my head again. In situations like this, the worst thing a person can do is be left alone to stew in their thoughts, and that is precisely what will be happening for the next week at least. This is a real low point for me. I begin to try and memorize Jesus' words about why we shouldn't worry, in Matthew 6.

FRIDAY 5 FEBRUARY

No patrols today either. Lots of rain though, and the camp soon becomes a complete quagmire. Cold, wet, windy. Can't get in touch with Danielle. An IED explodes close to the base, a large, dark cloud mushrooming into the grey sky. A British convoy has been hit, but nobody is injured.

SATURDAY 6 FEBRUARY

Patrol into the local area today. Looking at the Afghan children running around in the cold mud with sandals, I try and remind myself that despite my current difficulties, life could be a lot worse. The patrol is thankfully quiet.

MONDAY 7 FEBRUARY

Sitting in Wahid for two days, I feel like I am slowly losing my mind, surrounded by people yet totally isolated. I call Thomas, thinking about handing in my notice—I don't know how I can do this for another year—but the signal cuts out, and I am not able to connect to him. I then feel bad for doing that. Wanting to escape from this situation isn't exactly putting trust in God, is it?

WEDNESDAY 9 FEBRUARY

A small push into a Taliban-held area today, to feel out how fierce the resistance will be during Moshtarak. As we wait in a compound, the all-familiar insurgent radio chatter escalates into nearby popping and crackling as they open fire. 'CRACK!' 'WHIZZ!' Bullets fly over the compound wall. Before, this would have been exciting, exhilarating. Now it is terrifying.

Another platoon of Estonian soldiers flank the Taliban and begin to engage their position. The incoming fire ceases immediately. We trudge back to base. This upcoming operation is not going to be fun.

THURSDAY 10 FEBRUARY

Fly back to Bastion. The operation will be launching from here in a few days. The Estonian and Afghan troops practice mounting and dismounting from a stationary Chinook, attempting to inject as much haste as they can into the routine. On mission launch day, there are going to be lots of helicopters and even more cogs in the machine—slick drills are vital to try and avoid any potentially lethal hold-ups.

FRIDAY 11 FEBRUARY

Film a speech from a British Brigadier to hundreds of men. I always imagine that officers that get to make speeches like this must make their contemporaries jealous—gigantic, historic operations don't happen every week.

SATURDAY 12 FEBRUARY

10.00 p.m.—Mission launch might be tomorrow. Call Danielle to say goodbye. Her mum answers the phone. I can hear agonized cries in the background. 'She's gone into premature labour,' her mum tells me. 'We are in an ambulance now on the way to the hospital.'

Breaking point. I sit down on a nearby tyre and begin to weep. This is absolutely brutal. I am about to be going into this operation, dropping into hostile territory—who knows what will happen—and now the woman I love has gone into hospital to have an almost dangerously premature birth! Is she going to give birth tonight? Is the father of the baby going to go along for the birth? Will he get to spend time with her and the baby? Where does that leave me? Will I even be alive in three days' time?

God, why have you let this happen now? It seems like a perfectly orchestrated plan to utterly crush me. Fighting off thoughts of Danielle in agonizing labour, I phone Mel to tell her about the situation—just needing someone to speak to—and then stumble back to my bed. In the medikit attached to my body armour, I have a spare fentanyl lollipop. They are designed for soldiers who have been injured, who can suck on it while they are in pain—it slowly releases fentanyl into their bloodstream, which calms them down. I feel it is unlikely that I will ever be in as much pain as I am now—and so I take out the spare one, lie back on my bed, and begin to suck on it while listening to trance music on my iPod. Before long, I descend into an uneasy sleep. Why do I feel like God has abandoned me?

SUNDAY 13 FEBRUARY

2.00 a.m.—Wake up. Instantly alert. Has she had the baby now? Is it over? I step outside to use the sat phone. No answer from Danielle's number. Try to call mum. Nothing. I am too awake now to go back to sleep. Trudge over to Estonian welfare room—it has an Internet connection.

Message Esther, my sister, asking if she has heard any news. A few minutes later, she replies that Danielle has not given birth, the doctors were able to stop her early labour.

Suddenly, Danielle comes online—what on earth? How can she be online in a hospital? She tells me that the church—bless them—had a whip round to see if anyone had a mobile internet USB stick, which would mean that Danielle could use a laptop in the hospital. I am so relieved that I could cry. She tells me that they put hormone patches on her belly that stopped the birth. She will be home soon.

12.00 noon—Mission launch confirmed to be tonight. Mel suggests that I ask Thomas if I can go home for a week of compassionate leave after this operation is completed. Thomas agrees—I could kiss them both for showing such kindness to me. My worries, darn them, now firmly centre on the operation. What if I don't make it?

A British soldier who is attached to the Estonians for the operation walks up to me. 'Hey Josh,' he says, pressing a small metal dog tag into my hand. 'I think this is yours, it has your name on it, mate.' I frown slightly, I haven't lost my tags—they are still firmly around my neck. I turn over the dog tag that he has given me, and I am lost for words. I can see why he thought it was mine; it has the word 'Joshua' written on it. It is a quotation from the Bible book of Joshua, the same verses that I repeated to myself over and over as I ran to help save Jon a year ago:

'Be strong and courageous. Do not be afraid; do not be discouraged, for the Lord your God will be with you wherever you go.' (Joshua 1:9)

Wow. There is no way that this can be chance. A soldier who I barely know, walking over to me and giving me this dog tag because—for all he knew—it belonged to me. These words from the Bible, God's promise coming at precisely this moment, when I needed it. The reminder that I shouldn't be afraid, because he will be with me wherever I go. If last night's utter misery—during which I began to doubt God—hadn't happened, then dear Mel and Thomas wouldn't have taken pity on me, and I wouldn't be going home in a few weeks. Now, out of nowhere, I might actually be there for the birth of the baby!

I feel that God has taught me a lesson here, to make a rather large understatement.

3.00 p.m.—Go for a run round Bastion. During the run, I pray and thank God for his amazing faithfulness, even despite my lack of trust in him last night. I decide that I am going to propose to Danielle when I get back home. Most people would probably say that I am mad for doing this fairly early into our relationship, but I want to demonstrate my commitment to Danielle and the baby, which might prove to be crucial in the difficult days of having a newborn baby around.

I surreptitiously find out Danielle's ring size from her mother, and make an order online. Time for bed, Operation Moshtarak begins tonight.

MONDAY 14 FEBRUARY

1.00 a.m.—Hundreds upon hundreds of soldiers congregate at a large staging area. We are in the second wave to deploy, and therefore we sit around, shivering, waiting for our turn. I lean on my back and try to sleep. Unsuccessful.

4.00 a.m.—The helicopters are back from dropping off the first wave. There are eight of them, hanging in the sky above us, their lights making them look like silent, ominous UFOs.

We receive the order to move out. I hoist my bag and begin to film the Afghan and Estonian soldiers in front of me boarding the Chinook. It is pitch black inside, and this is probably the largest number of people I have ever seen in a Chinook. Take off.

It's a short flight to the LZ. Two minutes to go. One minute. Landing. Two lines of soldiers run off the ramp and into the dark field. I jump off, and find myself knee deep in thick mud. Judging by the swearing and

Soldiers queue up to board a helicopter. They are about to launch Operation Moshtarak.

slipping sounds going on around me, quite a few people are bogged down. It takes five minutes to fully extricate everyone.

We begin to walk toward our objective, a small town fairly near Wahid, where the Estonians and Afghan forces will be putting in a checkpoint.

1.00 p.m.—No sign of any Taliban. It has been slow progress, with a backbreaking load. At every lengthy stop, I find myself dozing off in the watery sunshine. It's actually quite a pleasant day.

4.00 p.m.—We enter the village. It's fairly close to the village we were in last year where the Taliban hammered us. This time, it's all smiles and laughter as local children flock out to greet us. I can tell that some soldiers, especially the newer ones, are slightly disappointed that they didn't get the excitement they had hoped for. I am perfectly happy. A theory is beginning to form in my head—the big operations always seem to be the quieter ones, as the Taliban choose not to engage overwhelming ISAF and Afghan forces. Instead they sit back, watch what the enemy does, and start to lay bombs and fire at smaller units later on.

6.00 p.m.—Bedded down in a compound. Completely uneventful day and, judging by the lack of gunshot sounds in the surrounding area, the British have also had a fairly easy time of it thus far. I call Danielle on the satellite phone—it's Valentine's Day, after all.

TUESDAY 15 FEBRUARY

Patrol in the local area today. Film the Afghan soldiers talking to the local men and playing with the local children. I am even able to remove my helmet to record myself talking to the camera—a year ago that would have been unheard of. Is this a sign of improvement in the area?

After about three hours of walking, I begin to lose focus and, as we wind our way through grassy fields and muddy banks, I begin to plan how to propose to Danielle.

WEDNESDAY 16 FEBRUARY

Another quiet patrol. I am beginning to feel that my work down here is coming to an end, that there are only so many shots of soldiers walking or talking to locals that I can meaningfully record.

THURSDAY 17 FEBRUARY

Heading back to Bastion today. I am going in the back of an Estonian vehicle to a field where a helicopter will pick some of us up for transportation.

As I approach the vehicle, an Estonian soldier says something to me. Due to a slight language barrier, I am unable to completely understand what he is saying. I smile, nod, and say 'OK!', hoping that it wasn't anything important. All I could pick up was '… but don't worry.' Worry about what? I climb into the back of the vehicle. There are four people sitting in there already. I say hello and sit down, before I realize that only one of the four is an Estonian. The others are Afghan men, blindfolded, with hands tied. Taliban prisoners. Oh, so that's what the helpful chap outside meant, then.

We begin to drive. The blindfold of the Talib opposite me slightly slips down as the vehicle judders around. I can see the cold glint of his eyes in the darkness, staring at me. Begin to feel very uncomfortable. The three prisoners are sitting on one side of the vehicle, the Estonian soldier and I on the other. There is about a meter-wide gap between us. The Estonian is holding a rifle. I begin to make nervous mental calculations. If all three were to spring forward at us at the same time—they aren't tied down—it is very unlikely that he would be able to bring his weapon to bear in time. Would they be able to throttle us with their tied hands? The Talib opposite continues to stare at me. I slowly reach to my belt, and draw out my penknife. I hold it under my legs and carefully pop the blade out, unseen. If they do go for us, I'll at least be able to attempt to put up a fight; I'll throw the camera at them with one hand, and attack with the other.

Ten minutes of dark driving. Ten minutes of staring. Ten minutes of coiled muscles, ready to spring into action. The vehicle stops. The door swings open. Light floods into the back. The prisoners are taken out by another Estonian, as their helicopter arrives. Thank goodness.

Climb aboard the helicopter. The floor around my seat is slick with a dark liquid. I slip slightly as I sit, and the hard plastic case carrying my portable satellite dish falls out of my hand. It hits a lump—which is covered in a thin poncho—with a soft thump. Horrific realization dawns on me. It's a dead body. And I've just dropped a box on its head. Feel awful. Judging by the trousers and boots, which peek out from beneath the poncho, it's an Afghan soldier. The dark liquid is now oozing around the soles of my boots. It's his blood.

Arrive back at Camp Bastion. Next year can't come soon enough.

FRIDAY 19 FEBRUARY

Text from Fahran. He wants to meet in Kabul today. He is understandably quite nervous about being out and about. I agree to meet him on a street corner this afternoon.

1.00 p.m.—I drive to the meeting point and pull up quickly. I see a man with a scarf covering his face, with sunglasses to hide his eyes. This must be Fahran. I dial Fahran's number, and I see the figure reaching for his phone. This is him. I open the door, he jumps in, and we speed off.

Fahran tells me about his life, a traumatic tale. His father had his throat slit in front of Fahran for being involved with Christian missionaries. Fahran then escaped the country and went to the UK as an illegal immigrant. He was found by the authorities, and taken to an immigration removal facility. While he was there, he had a powerful dream about a cross coming out of a large body of water, and a voice said to him 'Your sins can be washed away'. Soon after, Fahran became a Christian and was baptized before being flown back here.

Fahran is now living in Kabul above a shop, ostracized from the rest of his family, who have threatened to kill him. In the light of his story, my problems really don't seem that bad at all. I spend time talking to and encouraging him. I have also brought some of my spare clothes, a sleeping bag, some food, and a torch for him. He has no possessions at all.

I ask him whether he worries about his future or not—I don't know how I would cope if I was faced with his situation. He replies 'Sometimes I worry, yes. But when I do, I remember that Jesus is my Lord, and that he has got a bright tomorrow all ready for me. It may not be in twenty-four hours, or even twenty-four years, but I know that he will bring me through to see brighter times, even if I don't get to see them in this life. That is why I do not worry.'

We pray together and say goodbye. He is going to be attempting to go to Austria soon. I hope he makes it.

TUESDAY 23 FEBRUARY

Mel and Ruth take me out to a Lebanese restaurant for my birthday. They are even able to source a chocolate cake to celebrate the occasion. They really are like a second family, and I'm so grateful to have them.

THURSDAY 4 MARCH

Back in Copenhagen, staying at David and Laura's flat. Flying to the UK tomorrow morning. I see in the news that a soldier in Sangin has been killed. Immediately I recognize the photo. It's Carlos, the South African guy at Blenheim who would frequently be seen dispensing his wisdom to the younger soldiers—advising them not to fritter away money socializing, but to invest instead; teaching them to plan for the future. In return, they would always rib him about his age. He was shot dead while on a patrol seven hundred meters east of Blenheim. He leaves behind a long-term girlfriend. Tragic.

FRIDAY 5 MARCH

Fly back to the UK. Danielle meets me at the airport. I grab her in a huge hug, and we have our first kiss. I am sure that I want to marry this girl, and after all we have been through in the last few weeks, this kiss has been a long time coming. I have to go back to Afghanistan next Wednesday, so we are praying that the baby comes in this small time frame. It's going to be tight.

SATURDAY 6 MARCH

Having been given a week together, almost out of nowhere, we try and do as much 'couple stuff' as we can before the baby comes. I am beginning to panic though—what if I have to go back before the baby arrives? Am I just setting myself up for another night of pain. Lord, please help us out here.

MONDAY 8 MARCH

Two days left. I am feeling despair slowly creeping over me. It doesn't look like it's going to happen. I try not to let my negative feelings show to Danielle, but I don't think I succeed very well.

2.00 p.m.—Appointment with the midwife. She gives us various tips to help the baby to come. Eating hot curry is one of them.

7.00 p.m.—Order a curry. No luck.

TUESDAY 9 MARCH

Propose to Danielle. I am sitting on a couch cuddling her, and I say 'If I could be sitting on a couch, cuddling you sixty years from now, then I would be a very happy person. The Bible says that "he who finds a wife finds a good thing and obtains favour from the Lord". Well, I want more than a "good thing", I want you, my soulmate. Will you marry me?' Danielle bursts into tears, and forgets to say yes for about ten minutes.

WEDNESDAY 10 MARCH

I am supposed to fly back to Denmark at 11.20 today. Thomas and Mel agree that me going back—and missing the birth—probably wouldn't be very productive for me. They agree to let me have another week at home. Thankful.

SATURDAY 13 MARCH

It's been an amazing week with Danielle, we feel like we are making up for lost time. The clock is ticking, however. If the baby is not here by Wednesday, I will have to go back.

SUNDAY 14 MARCH

No baby. Is this going to happen? Trying to fight off despair and trust in God. I am still holding onto the dog tag that the British soldier gave me. No fear. No discouragement. Just faith. Wednesday is only a few days away, though.

MONDAY 15 MARCH

5.00 p.m.—Contractions. Could this be it? I am careful—there have been several false alarms this week, I don't want to wreck my morale my allowing myself to hope too much.

7.00 p.m.—Contractions. Real ones. They are increasing in frequency and pain, judging by Danielle's exclamations.

11.00 p.m.—Contractions are severe now. I try to comfort her by rubbing her arm, but I am verbally and physically beaten back, a lesson that every man has to learn. We are still in Danielle's parents' house—the church house that I used to live in. It feels extremely odd to be experiencing this here; I spent seventeen years of my life in this building.

Mum comes over, and we take her to hospital. The nurses tell us that Danielle's body isn't ready yet, and that we must go home. Really? She is in agony. We return home.

Danielle sits in the bath with her mum beside her. I am outside, lying on the floor of the hallway. I read my Bible and pray. It's hard to keep track of time, this is all very surreal.

TUESDAY 16 MARCH

4.00 a.m.—There is a 'pop' from the bathroom. 'Her waters have broken!' Danielle's mum, Melody, shouts. Here we go, then. We take Danielle into her bedroom, which, incidentally, also used to be my bedroom. The surreal element of the occasion has just tripled. Seeing that we aren't married yet, I try to focus on Danielle's face, leaving Melody to look at the other areas. 'I can see his head! His hair is coming out!' she says. Panic. The baby is coming now, no time for hospital. Phone Mum—who is a doctor—and tell her to come round now. I also dial 999 and ask for an ambulance. The baby continues its voyage into the world.

Mum arrives, followed minutes later by the ambulance crew. Because we are not in hospital, there are very few painkillers that can be given to Danielle, who has to make do with the unsubstantial gas and air pain relief that is on offer. Watching her sweat, scream, and push, I have a moment of profound clarity: I am glad that God made me a man.

Baby Jacob is now fully out. A paramedic hands me a pair of medical scissors and asks if I want to cut the cord. This is a huge honour, most fathers don't get the chance when the birth occurs in hospital. The ambulance crew is ecstatic; they rarely get to deliver babies. Danielle and I look at each other, tears glistening in our eyes. It's done. The baby is finally here.

Danielle sleeps, and I look at the baby boy swaddled in his crib. I read him the story of Jacob in the Bible and watch him sleep. I can't believe this is happening.

I am supposed to be flying back to Kabul tomorrow, but because the baby has just arrived, Thomas kindly agrees to let me have an extra week with Danielle and baby Jacob. I look back on my fear and doubt; I cannot help but laugh. Beyond all hope, God granted me two weeks of time alone with Danielle, and then an extra week with the baby. All of this, because of the early labour.

Josh holding baby Jacob.

FRIDAY 19 MARCH

Baby Jacob has reflux and colic—both of which only affect a small proportion of babies, but create much distress for the poor little chap. He cries for most of the day—I am sure that the screams are slowly murdering my brain cells—and it's quite a relief when I go home at night. I suddenly have a newfound respect for every woman who has ever been a mother—doing this is very tough. If a genie was to appear and offer me a choice between getting shot at or a day with a screaming baby, I think I'd choose the former.

WEDNESDAY 24 MARCH

I say goodbye to Danielle. Despite the tears—it's slightly easier this time—we are both completely shattered from the rigours of wrangling a newborn and, in fairness to Danielle, I think that she needs space to bond with the baby and focus on him. Having me there adds an extra

distraction at a rather bad time. I kiss her and Jacob goodbye, and head off
to the airport.

13 Spring

2 April 2010—12 May 2010

FRIDAY 2 APRIL

Down in Kandahar, waiting for a flight. I am hoping to go to Arghandab—the area where Dan had a close call in 2008—with a US battalion. Flights have been cancelled every day thus far and it isn't looking good. Second of April today. Danielle and I have agreed to get married on 2 April next year, as I will have been back from Afghanistan for a few weeks by then. One year to go. Trying not to think about how long a time 365 days actually is.

SUNDAY 4 APRIL

Trip cancelled, back to Kabul.

MONDAY 5 APRIL

Arrive back. Because my trip has fallen through, Mel asks if I could go straight out to the east—via the dreaded Bagram Airbase—on an embed with some US infantry soldiers in Logar province. After the ordeal of sitting in KAF for a week, alone with my thoughts, I am not overly keen to go straight back out again. Since meeting Danielle, I am finding this aspect of my life the hardest in which to honour God—having a good attitude about going on things that I really don't want to.

THURSDAY 8 APRIL

Arrive at a small outpost in Logar, which is situated in a green valley between two looming ridgelines. The Taliban have been running a fairly comprehensive intimidation campaign against the local people, which the US soldiers based here are finding difficult to combat. My first patrol is tomorrow.

FRIDAY 9 APRIL

2.00 p.m.—Patrol into the nearby town to talk to the local shop owners about the 'night letters' that the Taliban keep sending. Night letters are a common form of intimidation. Taliban fighters go into population centres and post these letters—which are usually lists of punishable offences. The locals become understandably terrified, and their level of cooperation with ISAF forces drops rapidly. Matt, the American lieutenant in charge of the patrol, waves a night letter—which his soldiers have torn off a shop wall—at the owner of the building. 'How can you not know about this?' Matt asks, seething with frustration. The shop owner claims that he has no knowledge of the Taliban, or how the letter got there. Judging by his

US and Afghan soldiers look at a night letter.

subdued expression—and the resentful looks of passers-by—I imagine that most of them actually have a very good idea about Taliban activity in this town.

The problem with night letters is that they are very hard to stop. Even if there is an ISAF base next to—or even inside—the town, it's very easy for the Taliban to sneak in and post them, thus winning the psychological battle. I can't see how, besides having troops covering every inch of the village twenty-four hours per day, this problem can be solved.

On the way through the bazaar, we see large packs of ammonium nitrate fertilizer being sold at several shops. Matt is incredulous. He asks the shop owners whether they know the Afghan government has banned this, as it can be used in bombs. The shopkeepers—as usual—deny all knowledge. The Afghan soldiers, who are accompanying Matt's patrol, begin to try and confiscate the sacks. There are so many of them, though, that the confiscation alone will be a fairly long-term process. As the Afghan soldiers walk away with the sacks in 'borrowed' wheelbarrows, I can feel the resentment building in this town.

6.00 p.m.—Finally heading back to base. Light is beginning to fade. 'WHHOOOOOOOSH! BOOOM!'; an RPG, aimed at the parting patrol from the direction of the town, flies toward us. It's a bit of a speculative shot, though, as the town is almost a kilometre away. The RPG detonates woefully short of our position. The intention behind it is clear, however: go away, this place belongs to the Taliban. I feel sorry for Matt and the soldiers with him. How on earth are they supposed to fight the insurgency here?

SUNDAY 11 APRIL

Hoping for a flight out of here today. Time is getting quite short. We are all supposed to be flying to Brussels this Wednesday, so that NATO HQ can (finally!) meet in person with the fools that run around in warzones with cameras on their behalf. Being in Europe would mean that I would be able to sneak home for a weekend with Danielle and Jacob. It all depends on getting a flight from here, though. It took several days for me to get from

Bagram to here, and therefore I would need everything to go smoothly in order to get me back to Kabul on time.

3.00 p.m.—Flight cancelled. Begin to feel slightly resentful of Mel—if she hadn't sent me on this trip, then I wouldn't have this problem. No, Josh, that's not a good attitude to have—why don't you start trusting God instead of allowing negative feelings to fester? Despite all that God has done for me in the past few months—all the expectations that have been defied, all the hopeless situations turned around—I still find it extremely doubtful that I will make it back on time.

MONDAY 12 APRIL

I am told that a helicopter is coming that will take me straight to Bagram. Excited. Board it. A piece of paper is passed to me, and I am asked to put my name next to the destination that I will be disembarking at. Bagram is not on the list. Oh no. I try to explain that I am supposed to be headed to Bagram. The American crewman shakes his head. They aren't going to Bagram, and now I am going to be dropped off at a random base. It's not looking good in terms of making it back to Kabul in time for the Brussels flight.

The helicopter flies a ring route, stopping at numerous bases. Passengers board and disembark. We end up at FOB Shank, a fairly large base where several aircraft are situated. The helicopter stops to refuel. I explain my predicament. The pilot is sympathetic. Another passenger comes forward; he was supposed to be going to Bagram too. 'Well,' says the pilot, 'I think that we might be able to arrange a detour for you.' I have never seen or heard of such a deviation from a routine flight happening here before. Result.

WEDNESDAY 14 APRIL

Depart from Kabul Airport. An Afghan airline, Safi, has started offering flights directly to and from Hamburg, in Germany. For all Europeans working in Afghanistan, this is great. The Danish support of NATO TV, in order to get it off the ground, has now ended—and thus the pleasant London to Copenhagen to Turkey to Afghanistan routine that I have become so accustomed to has come to an end.

Board the flight with Mel, Will, and Ruth. Afghan planes have a fairly wonky reputation, but this one seems to be very nice. Safi, realizing the Western concerns about Afghan aviation, seems to have bought foreign aircraft and employed European pilots. Can't say that I complain. There's plenty of space on the aircraft, and we all stretch out. Looking around at my friends, it's an odd feeling. A fairly luxurious 747 is far too normal for the various locations that I have become used to seeing them in. We have become truly Afghan-ized.

5.00 p.m.—Land in Brussels, having gone via Hamburg. NATO puts us up in a nice hotel near HQ. Sitting on the soft sheets of the bed, it's hard to think that this morning I woke up in Afghanistan.

THURSDAY 15 APRIL

Lots of meetings at NATO today. I count down the hours until I see Danielle tomorrow.

FRIDAY 16 APRIL

More meetings. Finally finish mid-afternoon. I am very glad that I booked Eurostar train tickets back to London instead of flying; a volcano in Iceland has erupted, and is creating travel havoc for people everywhere.

7.00 p.m.—Arrive back in London. A nice, film-esque reunion with Danielle on the platform of our local train station. Go back to her house and see baby Jacob, who seems to have grown so much already.

SATURDAY 17 APRIL

I wonder if this volcano is going to disrupt my flight back to

Afghanistan. I have Eurostar tickets booked to go back to Brussels on Monday, but if there is no flight, surely there is no point going back to Belgium just yet?

SUNDAY 18 APRIL

Flights everywhere are cancelled. I don't think I have ever been so grateful for a natural disaster. Mel suggests that I may as well take a few weeks of holiday. It means that I will have to do almost five months straight in Afghanistan come summer, but I am happy to be home for now.

THURSDAY 22 APRIL

Jacob's father, Danielle's ex, visits today. He has asked to visit every week. Wanting to do the right thing, and not shut him out, Danielle has agreed to it. Despite the fact that I know it is the right and Christian thing to do, I absolutely hate it. The idea of him coming round and sitting with the baby, in Danielle's house, for several hours—especially when I am back in Afghan—kills me. I try to swallow my feelings, and attempt to talk about work and football; normal 'guy stuff'. It's a frighteningly awkward affair. Being stuck out there for so long this summer, knowing these visits are going on, is really going to hurt.

MONDAY 26 APRIL

Jacob's colic means that from about five o'clock in the afternoon, through to ten o'clock in the evening, he screams. And screams. And screams. It is incredible to think that something so small can create such noise. Danielle's mum kindly agrees to look after him a couple of times per week so Danielle and I can have some alone time. Even walking around the block together in the evening feels amazing—just to be outside, away from the crying. He is a very cute baby though. Being male, I try to look past the newborn stage to the times in the future when I can play football with him.

TUESDAY 11 MAY

Tolkien describes an imminent goodbye as 'the shadow of parting'—a phrase that joins the elephant in mine and Fred's lexicon of emotional shorthand. Now the shadow lies heavily upon me, sucking the vibrancy and joy out of life and replacing it with an ever-increasing sadness. I am looking forward to the day when there are no more goodbyes.

Danielle and I make the most of our last evening together and go for a nice meal. Under every word, glance, thought, and action lays the fact that I am about to go away for almost five months—my longest unbroken stint in Afghanistan thus far. Add to that already heartbreaking recipe the fact that Danielle's ex will be visiting every week, the difficulties of having a newborn child, and the fact that I might well be in danger, and we have a mighty cocktail of absolute despair. 'How are we going to get through this?' Danielle asks me. I answer that we must trust in God. Usually, answers like this can often be half-felt; a fall back reply that can roll off the tongue so easily, when the actual implications of following such a statement are enormous. This time, though, I am being completely serious. I have no other strength to rely on right now.

WEDNESDAY 12 MAY

Usual heart-rending goodbye. Back to war.

14 133 Days

13 May 2010—22 September 2010

THURSDAY 13 MAY

Arrive back in Kabul. Mel, Ruth, and Will are all away at the moment, so it's quite quiet. Call Danielle to let her know I have arrived safely. She tells me that her ex visited yesterday. Instead of spending time with his son, Jacob, he spent most of the visit making an impassioned plea that she get back together with him. My blood boils. Did he deliberately wait until I was out of the picture on the other side of the world to try it on? I ask God to help me not to hate him for it. It's very difficult.

My strategy for this summer stretch, a regrettable one hundred and thirty-three days, is not to have a countdown. In previous stints here this year, I have been running on one. I realized how selfish that was of me when Mel mentioned how it was slightly hurtful to the team, as it appears that I am wishing away all my time out there. She was totally right, and I resolve not to do it this time. I will try and take each day as it comes, trusting in God to give me what I need to get through this time. Besides, the World Cup is on soon, and I love football. It's being held in South Africa. Danielle is South African. Cue instant pain again. Argh.

SATURDAY 22 MAY

Email from Fahran. He has managed to escape to Austria, taking his sister with him. He is being held there while the authorities decide whether to deport him or not. He asks me to provide a letter of reference, citing his need. I do so, explaining a bit about his situation, and ending the letter with 'I am not sure how the decision-making process in Austria works, but I would urge you in the strongest possible terms to prevent Fahran's return to Afghanistan. If he does come back here, I would estimate that he wouldn't live to see 2011.'

I send the letter to him to print out and give to the relevant person. I hope he gets to stay in Europe.

TUESDAY 1 JUNE

Down in Kandahar, waiting for a flight to Camp Nathan Smith, the Canadian base in the middle of the city that I spent some time in during December 2008.

Text from Ruth. Her dad has just died—apparently collapsing while out at the shops. She is frantically trying to get a flight back to the UK tonight. I think back to the beginning of my time here, when I thought that my mum had the stroke—it was horrific, and that wasn't even death. I can't even imagine what Ruth must be going through. In light of Ruth and Fahran's current situations, I really don't have it bad at all.

WEDNESDAY 2 JUNE

At HLS, waiting for a flight to Camp Nathan Smith. I think back to my last trip there, and all that has gone on since—it feels like so long ago now.

Nearby, a Chinook lands and US Special Forces walk off the ramp—beards, sunglasses, the very latest equipment. They have several prisoners with them. Everybody in the queue for my helicopter seems to shrink a bit. It's interesting how men—including myself—react in the face of genuine alpha males.

THURSDAY 3 JUNE

I am slightly disgusted at Camp Nathan Smith, which is known as 'CNS' to the residents. Like some of the Italian bases I have visited, the soldiers here live in relative luxury. Last time I was here, it was December, and the true decadence of the base failed to shine through. Now, in the hot summer sun, the swimming pool, the deck chairs, the parasols, and the piles of free fruit create a bizarre 'holiday camp' atmosphere. I can't decide whether to be happy about this or not. Immediately, and on a rather selfish level, it's nice to be at a place like this. On the other hand, as I felt at 'Camp Lobster' in Herat, it just seems very dishonourable when so many soldiers in Kandahar and Helmand are living in squalor, under daily attack.

WEDNESDAY 7 JUNE

Have spent the week conducting fairly meaningless patrols with the Canadian soldiers. Any novelty that came with having a swimming pool and fruit has now dried up. This is not the way to fight a war.

FRIDAY 11 JUNE

Despite being on a rather high horse about how good soldiers have it here at CNS, I am rather glad when the World Cup begins and I have access to a TV.

WEDNESDAY 16 JUNE

Back in Kabul, editing the stories that I filmed with the Canadians down in CNS. Every night, after work is done, I head over to the British NSE to watch the football. There are several different NSEs in the immediate vicinity—German, Italian, Dutch—to name a few—and it's very entertaining hearing the cheers or groans from a neighbouring building when their respective team scores or concedes a goal.

TUESDAY 20 JUNE

Britney the cat, who we think is George's sister, walks into the office with a bird in her mouth. Not sure if it is alive or dead, I gently grab her in a headlock and prize the poor little chap out. It's one of the small sparrows we see often around our base. It's still alive, relatively unharmed.

Seizing the chance, it suddenly takes off and makes a bid for the door. A tabby-coloured blur flies past my head and grabs the bird. Oh Britney.

Headlock rescue again. Once more, the bird is unharmed, but now in a serious state of shock. I put it in a plastic box to let it recover. Will, in his great tradition of random animal names, decides that the bird should be called 'Superfluous'. Not sure why.

After about an hour, Superfluous seems finally ready to leave. As he flies out of the box, George appears from nowhere and catches him. Devastated at poor Superfluous' run of luck, I throw myself at George, and am able to extricate the bird. I am surprised that it hasn't had a heart attack yet. Three 'in-mouth' experiences in one day would test the sternest of creatures.

We lock George and Britney—siblings in crime—in the office while we finally let Superfluous go. He flies off, decidedly cheerful. I hope he has the sense to avoid this area from now on.

THURSDAY 22 JUNE

Fly down to a large shura in Kandahar with General McChrystal. Trips like this are always a short straw, but the fact that it is with him makes it slightly more bearable.

The shura is being held in the basement of a building here. Hundreds of Afghan officials and ISAF officers are crammed in, and it's a dreary affair. The Afghans love making long speeches, in which the initial greeting part can take up to ten minutes and, of course, everything has to be translated. The fierce June heat slowly cooks us all down here. Even McChrystal looks weary of it by the end. We are glad to finally fly back to Kabul.

As we touch down at HQ ISAF, two US soldiers run over to McChrystal's Black Hawk and give him an urgent message. He stays aboard the helicopter, which soon lifts off, carrying him in the direction of Kabul airbase. I wonder what that was all about.

11.00 p.m.—Sitting in the office with Mel. She likes to have a news channel running whenever we are in there, to keep us up to date with what is happening around the world (and perhaps it's her secret design that some of the journalistic skill we see and hear will rub off on Will and I).

Reports suddenly start to come through that McChrystal has been summoned back to Washington, and is in big trouble with President Obama. What is going on here?

FRIDAY 23 JUNE

McChrystal has been sacked. An article, which is about to be published in *Rolling Stone* magazine, contains alleged comments made by McChrystal and his staff that are disparaging toward the White House. Obama has little choice but to sack him, but it's quite a devastating blow to everybody here. McChrystal was an inspirational leader. I am sure though, that some will be happy. The general, in an attempt to streamline the military effort here—and perhaps to make the rear base soldiers more disciplined like him—was keen to shut down some of the various amenities in the bases around the country, the KAF boardwalk being one of them. I have heard some soldiers complain about this. None of them, however, ever have to go and fight. Goodbye, General.

SUNDAY 27 JUNE

Preaching in the chapel tonight. It's a fairly packed affair—gone are the days of preaching to ten people in a wooden shack—and I am faced with a bit of a challenge. I am preaching about putting God first in everything, but, to my horror, I find out that England are scheduled to play Germany in the knockout stages of the World Cup while our church service takes place. Games like this are usually fairly historic affairs, but I resolve to follow the words of my sermon and put God first. When the service is finally finished, I head over to the British NSE to see what the score is. I am told the Germans are winning by four goals to one. German soldiers, in their nearby NSE, are crowing triumphantly.

SUNDAY 4 JULY

General David Petraeus—widely credited for being 'the man who won the Iraq war for America'—has arrived today, after being asked personally by President Obama to take over the command of ISAF after General

McChrystal's sacking. Despite his reputation, and the fact he is more media-savvy than McChrystal, I don't see how Petraeus can command the same amount of respect among the troops as his predecessor did. He is physically smaller, and fainted while in front of Congress last week. We will see.

MONDAY 5 JULY

Danielle has decided that it's probably best that she doesn't tell me specifically when her ex is visiting Jacob, as it just creates lots of worries in my head. Despite the wisdom of this move, I find that I resort to a hopeless guessing game and try to work it out anyway. I am beginning to think that I am going slightly crazy here.

TUESDAY 13 JULY

I accompany General Petraeus—known as 'P4' by his staff—on his first battlefield tour. He chooses to go to Kandahar, which is fast becoming my 'frequent flier location' of the summer, where he will be visiting some of his troops. His personal media handler, an American soldier called Eric, sidles up to me grinning. 'I hope you can keep up with him, he moves pretty fast!' he says. I am unsure what to say, I don't imagine that 'P4' will be running everywhere, surely. I think that Eric's comment was just an insult directed at us media types, who might not be physically fit enough to walk very fast. I decide to brush it off—there has been a fair amount of anti-media sentiment since McChrystal's sacking, which is understandable.

2.00 p.m.—We arrive at one of the bases. Petraeus, walking at a normal speed, goes into the briefing room with the officers here and begins to talk to them. I begin to film him; a shot of him with 'the men' will look good in the story that I will be cutting together. He suddenly spots me, and jabs a finger at me. 'Are you press?' he demands angrily. Everybody in the room—about one hundred US soldiers—turns and glares at me. If looks could kill. I wish that the floor would swallow me up. 'No sir, I'm internal media', I say meekly. I stop filming anyway—the hate toward media in this room is too strong for me to dare doing anything else.

THURSDAY 22 JULY

After a fairly mission-less couple of months, it's time for me to head down to Kandahar (where else?) for a long trip. Ruth and I walk to the car, past George the cat, who is hanging in a camouflage net attempting to scalp any unwary passers-by. Ruth drops me at Kabul Airbase.

This summer, Kandahar seems to have become 'the new Helmand' in terms of media interest, as there is a large, yet slow-paced operation happening here. Due to the rather anti-climactic nature of Operation Khanjar last summer, and Operation Moshtarak in February—both in terms of actual fighting and less-than-desired-impact achieved—this Kandahar effort is all about slowly flooding in troops to increase the ISAF presence. There are some here who wonder why this didn't happen sooner, seeing that the city—the second largest in Afghanistan—is seen symbolically as the home of the Taliban. It was in that area that Mullah Omar, the infamous one-eyed cleric, started the Talib movement.

Fly down to KAF. To my disappointment, I find out that I will be spending the first part of my trip back at CNS again. The Canadians are beginning to pull out of Afghanistan, leaving the Americans to take up the slack, and CNS is slowly being handed over to US control. This seems likely to herald the end of the holiday camp lifestyle, much to the chagrin of the few Canadians that remain.

SUNDAY 25 JULY

I am taken on a tour of some police checkpoints surrounding Kandahar city. The Afghan National Police (ANP) are partnering with US military police, who are endeavouring to teach their new colleagues about policing.

Dripping with sweat, I go on a joint patrol with the US Army and the ANP around a small village on the outskirts of Kandahar. I am slightly disappointed with the ANP, who saunter along like members of the mafia, harassing some local men about a motorbike. The Americans have to step in to resolve the situation. The future of the country—and indeed the whole ISAF withdrawal plan—rests on the competency of the Afghan security forces. From what I have seen during my time here, I think that there are going to be some real difficulties.

FRIDAY 29 JULY

Leave CNS for good—phew—and go to a small FOB with US paratroopers who, like the military police, are partnering with police. I am told that the police here are different. They belong to the Afghan National Civil Order Police, or ANCOP, and are supposedly better trained, more motivated, and less corrupt than their brethren in the ANP. I take this claim with a pinch of salt, but it will be interesting to patrol with them.

SATURDAY 30 JULY

Go on a patrol with ANCOP and US soldiers. The ANCOP lieutenant, a chap from northern Afghanistan, leads the patrol. I double take as I see him actually leading it, not sauntering along in a relaxed fashion. His men conduct themselves in a professional, alert manner. He even gets a notepad out and begins writing as a local man conveys a grievance. Despite my growing cynicism, this is actually very impressive. If only there were ANCOP everywhere.

WEDNESDAY 4 AUGUST

I accompany a colonel named David for two days as he shows me the work done by his men at various areas around Kandahar. Being usually rather cynical about officers of his rank—or higher—I am immediately impressed by David. He shows a real compassion for his men, even when admonishing them. I see him helping some low ranking soldiers put up a large camouflage net. He isn't doing this for the camera, I am not filming, and I don't even think that he knows I am watching him. He is a real example of leadership through service, a quality I have rarely seen from those in command.

At dinner, I see him sit down. He bows his head in prayer to say grace. It all makes sense now. I walk over to him. 'Sir, are you a Christian?' He smiles and nods. We sit and talk, comparing notes for about half an hour. It's a real privilege to meet him. I wish him all the best with the rest of his tour.

MONDAY 9 AUGUST

My final stop of this Kandahar trip is something that I have wanted to do for years out here: an embed with the American crews that fly the medevac helicopters to rescue wounded soldiers. Theirs is a glamorous job—they command the respect of all the troops out here—and, in a place where purposes and meanings are often questioned, they really can say that they make a difference. I watched the film *Black Hawk Down* last night, probably not the best way to prepare myself for flying in Black Hawk helicopters all week, but I just find the vehicles fascinating, awe-inspiring.

The crew that I am going to be spending the week with are about to fly out to FOB Ramrod, which is based in Maiwand—near where I did my very first mission with the Paras in 2008—to relieve the medevac crew who are stationed there. Crews are rotated fairly regularly to keep everyone fresh.

We fly out to Ramrod, and the new crew takes over. Now we just sit and wait. It's an odd way of life. Whenever a medevac call comes in, the crew members have to be in their helicopters, off the ground, within seven minutes. The doctrine for saving wounded people states that if they are in hospital within an hour of being wounded, the survival ratio is much higher. This is called 'the golden hour', and the quick deployment of the medevac rescue teams is integral to keeping within this timeframe.

Because of this, everybody has to carry a radio around with them, ready for the 'Medevac! Medevac! Medevac!' call that will send them springing into action. Everything suddenly takes on a new element of risk—the simple act of having a shower now becomes an assessment—are we likely to get called out as soon as I am stripped out of my clothes? When we go to eat, we eat in one big group, with several radios on the table. We get to jump any queues. We spend the time sitting in a tent, talking, watching

DVDs, playing cards, on Skype to loved ones. It's an odd existence. It's Ramadan at the moment, and there are no medevac calls today. I spend the time trying to ingratiate myself with the crew, and finding out about them.

Dave, one of the pilots, is an easy-going southerner who has been around in the Army for years. He even used to fly in the famed 'Night Stalkers', a unit of Special Forces pilots that are tasked with flying elite SF troops into combat. He is very friendly, and we get on well.

Luke, the other pilot, is a softly spoken young guy who I also find out is a Christian. He carries a maturity about him that belies his age. This is his first deployment to a war zone, and he is soaking up information from Dave as fast as he can.

Audrey is the primary medic, who travels in the back of the helicopter. It's her job to deal with the casualties. If being the only woman on the team phases her, she doesn't show it, exchanging easy banter and jokes with the other guys, who seem to regard her with tremendous respect. I am told that her medical skills are 'epic'.

Chad is the last member of the team. He is the crew chief, and sits in the back of the helicopter with Audrey. He is in charge of the logistics of the chopper—he decides when we can get out, he handles the refuelling, provides cover for Audrey with his rifle, and sorts out various other important things. I think he has a slight distrust of me, and is a bit standoffish.

Laing, Justin, Howard, and Rameesh are the crew for the other Black Hawk, the 'chase bird'. The job of the chase bird—which is armed—is to follow the 'med bird' and provide covering fire for it as it rescues the wounded.

TUESDAY 10 AUGUST

No medevac calls today. I also discover that the tent is stocked with all manner of food—so that the crew could stay here, ready to go, if need be. Someone could really pick up weight here if they aren't careful, what with the limitation of movement and abundant supply of food. I speak to Danielle on Skype, and see Jacob. He seems to be really growing up. The colic is slowly beginning to go, which is a huge relief for us both. He is dressed in a little green monster suit. Very cute.

WEDNESDAY 11 AUGUST

6.00 a.m.—We are all asleep. The radio crackles into life 'Medevac! Medevac! Medevac!' Everybody jumps. I am amazed at the speed with which they throw their boots on—they all sleep fully clothed except for footwear—and run out the door. I stumble after them, the transition from pitch-black tent to bright Afghan sunlight blinding me, my laces dragging in the dirt as I run with the camera. The Black Hawk begins to whine as Dave and Luke begin the start-up procedure. We take off within minutes.

It's a fairly short flight. The injuries have been categorized as 'CAT A'— the most serious grade of injury, needing immediate evacuation. We touch down in a small FOB, and two stretchers are placed aboard. They both bear Afghan men. One has a long dark beard, and eyeliner on. Wait a second, is he- 'Taliban,' says Audrey, answering my unspoken question. I know that ISAF, under the Geneva Convention, is required to treat enemy combatants, but to see it happen for real is mad. Audrey carefully tends to him—he is wrapped in a foil sheet to preserve body heat—and I am unable to see what his injuries are. I wonder what would happen if the Taliban came across a wounded ISAF soldier. I doubt, somehow, that they would be extended the same courtesy.

THURSDAY 12 AUGUST

Two more medevac calls today. It's all been Afghans so far. When the radio call comes in, the crackle of static that briefly precedes the message usually has everybody jumping up before the word 'Medevac!' is even out. The slight problem with this is that there tend to be several harmless, unimportant messages that come throughout the day, and which play absolute havoc with our nerves and adrenal glands.

The Medevac Black Hawk in action.

FRIDAY 13 AUGUST

Sitting on the toilet. Always a gamble, especially because I am radio-less—there simply aren't enough to go around. As I sit there, I hear a distant noise. Is that the sound of the Black Hawk starting up? Faint whining noise. Oh goodness. Finish my business and run out of the toilet—belt loose, wearing only a t-shirt and combat trousers. Make it to the helicopter just in time, mildly embarrassed.

SATURDAY 14 AUGUST

I show the team some of my combat footage—especially the footage involving medevac rescues. They all seem to really enjoy it—it's probably interesting for them to see what life is like on the front line, and how a situation unfolds when they are called in. I am really enjoying this week with them; they are a great bunch of people, and I begin to wish that I could have done more embeds like this in my time here. Even Chad

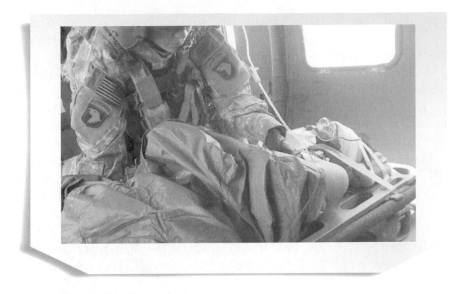

Audrey tending to a wounded Afghan.

has softened toward me, asking me for advice on some photos that he has taken.

SUNDAY 15 AUGUST

I am becoming quite quick at reacting and running to the helicopter. Another call today sends us roaring into action. As we begin to take off, Chad turns to me and says 'We are going into a hot LZ!' A hot LZ means that there is high probability of enemy action as we try to land. We lift off. I try not to think about *Black Hawk Down*.

We arrive at a small FOB, which is under attack from the Taliban. As we swoop over, I can see the small puffs of dust which indicate gunfire. It seems so peaceful from up here. Dave steers us in, and we land with a bump. US soldiers rush out, carrying a stretcher. We don't want to be on the ground for long here. The wounded person is placed inside. It's an Afghan soldier who is seriously injured. He has been shot in the face, and is missing part of his hand, as well as suffering other shrapnel wounds to the torso. Audrey immediately hunches over him and begins to work. After a few minutes, there is little more that she can do, so she just holds his hand and tries to comfort him.

We land at KAF, which has a large hospital dedicated to the Afghan police and army. I jump in the ambulance as we travel between the HLS and hospital building. Afghan orderlies meet us at the ambulance, and rush the patient inside. Audrey conducts a handover, via an interpreter, with Afghan doctors.

As we fly back to Ramrod, I wonder what sort of life the Afghan soldier will have. I don't image that the medical care afforded to wounded Afghans is anything remotely like the level of care that we enjoy in the west. Every single medevac that we have conducted this week has been to rescue an Afghan. There are far more Afghan people wounded—many of them locals who accidentally set off a Taliban IED—than there are ISAF soldiers. Few people back home realize this, though. These are the true casualties of this war.

MONDAY 16 AUGUST

It's time for the team to rotate back to KAF. I travel with them, and bid them farewell. It's sad to leave them—of all the things I have done in Afghanistan, this week was one of my favourites.

10.00 p.m.—Fly back to Kabul. It's good to see the team again, especially Will, who picks me up. My method of not counting the days seems to be working—I will be home with Danielle in just over a month.

SUNDAY 21 AUGUST

At chapel, the Chaplain makes an impassioned plea for anyone with musical abilities to get involved in the musical side of the service. The keyboard player and guitarist—both of whom are brilliant—are finally rotating back to the US, leaving a gap. I remember that years ago, I used to play the guitar. I suppose I could give it a try. The fact that I—and I

The crew. From left: Luke, Chad, Josh, Audrey and Dave.

consider myself 'musically backward'—have to step forward shows what dire straits we are in.

WEDNESDAY 25 AUGUST

Band practice at chapel. As suspected, I am a fairly tragic guitar player. Thankfully, a US Air Force guitarist and a Romanian soldier have come forward also. When we get to the bit that I can't play, I just strum the air, and hope that their noise covers my lack of ability.

THURSDAY 2 SEPTEMBER

The final hurdle before I go home will be covering the Afghan parliamentary elections in a few weeks. The last election, the presidential one, turned out to be a bit of a fiasco—there were numerous reports of fraud on the day, and the ongoing argument was only resolved when President Karzai's chief opponent dropped out of the running.

I am hoping that the parliamentary elections will be quieter. The aim of these is to select the members of the Afghan Parliament, not the president himself.

MONDAY 6 SEPTEMBER

I accompany Ruth on the way to film an Afghan music school for children and teenagers. Ruth, being very musical herself, is very passionate about music amongst the Afghans, and has made some good contacts here. I have come along to be her cameraman, as she might be too busy talking to her contacts to do all the filming.

As we drive there in a taxi, a large white Toyota screeches up alongside us. Our taxi driver, not being the most sensible person in the world, attempts to cut in front of the white Toyota. An Afghan man leans out of the window and points an AK-47 rifle at us. My heart skips a beat. Are we about to be gunned down in a road rage incident? Ruth and I both shout at our errant driver to move out of the way. The gunman glares at us, and then disappears back into the car. It was the NDS, the shadowy Afghan equivalent of the FBI.

As my time in Afghanistan slowly winds to an end, I am finding myself becoming increasingly worried that I am going to get killed by an Afghan soldier, policeman, or NDS official. The idea of this worries me far more than the threat of the Taliban.

SATURDAY 18 SEPTEMBER

Afghan parliamentary election day. I go out to various polling stations around Kabul, and collect footage of the voters. The Afghan police at the stations I visit seem to be fairly relaxed, which is a huge relief. No sign of the Taliban, either. I just want to do this and get out of here.

WEDNESDAY 22 SEPTEMBER

Finally, the long summer is over. I stand at the Afghan airport, about to check in. We have to fly civilian since the Danish support was cut, an experience that I do not enjoy. As people working for ISAF, we are not required to have a visa. Well, that's supposed to be the rule. It all seems to depend on the temperament of the specific Afghan border guard handling the case. This time as I try to leave the country, the Afghan asks me for a bribe. Not wanting to give him any money, and desperate to get out of here, I give him a pen. It seems to work. Fly to Dubai. Next stop, London. Thank you Lord for getting me through this summer.

15 Final Stretch

2 October 2010—13 January 2011

SATURDAY 2 OCTOBER

Being home is amazing. Jacob is now able to sit up and shuffle around on his rear. Everything he gets his hands on goes in his mouth. I begin to seriously think about the future—what is it going to be like being a fulltime dad? I used to think that I would make a good dad, but in a sudden moment of clarity, I have realized that there is more to being a father than just playing football or having fun times with your child. I will be responsible for his upbringing—what he does, how he turns out, the man he grows up to be—all this will be influenced by how I father him. It's terrifying.

FRIDAY 15 OCTOBER

Danielle's birthday. I take her and Jacob to the London Aquarium for the day. In hindsight, it was probably a bit of a waste of money taking Jacob, seeing as he slept through most of it, and seemed largely uninterested by the fish on show, but it was a lovely day to spend together as a family. A taste of things to come.

The infernal elephant and its shadow, as usual, hang over everything we do. Going back to Afghanistan next week. God willing, it will be our last goodbye in this whole horrendous experience. Thomas, in a wonderful display of magnanimity, has lined up some work for me in to do back in the UK come January. I no longer have to push my time in Afghanistan out until March or April next year. January is the finish line.

WEDNESDAY 20 OCTOBER

This is it. On the way to the airport, I repeat to myself that we will not be doing this again. Just one more goodbye. My dear old grandmother, as well as my younger brother, Jared, accompany Mum, Danielle, Jacob, and I to the airport. It seems to be a small crowd, urging on an athlete to one final effort. Danielle and I, once more unable to remain dry-eyed, say goodbye to each other. Thankfully, Jacob is too interested in looking at the fluorescent lights to truly appreciate the gravity of the situation.

I walk away from the tearful group, with an awful feeling hanging over my head. What if this is like one of those films when a policeman, about to retire, takes on 'just one more case', and ends up paying for it with his life?

As I board the plane, I remind myself of my verse, that very special passage from the book of Joshua. God has been with me thus far. He has done so, so much for me. I know that whatever I face over the next three months, he will be with me, and that he will not forsake me. It is a very encouraging thing to know, especially because it looks like my final mission will be in Helmand.

THURSDAY 28 OCTOBER

Preparing to fly down to Helmand later on today. The plan is for me to spend a few weeks with the Danish troops in Gereshk, and then switch over to the British Paras, as they have rotated back to Afghanistan. It seems to be a fitting end to my Afghan experience—I have developed a great love for the Danes after all my experiences with them and their beautiful country over these past few years, and it will be great to do some final patrols with them. Finishing off with the Paras creates a wonderful symmetry; the first and last trips of my whole Afghan experience, with the regiment I used to belong to. It feels right.

I am nervous about being in Helmand, so close to the end now. I am assailed by worries and fears of what could happen to me, but I resolve to push them firmly to the side. God has got me this far, and has kept me safe in everything I have done. I am not going to shy away from Helmand, I am going to let it be an act of trust in him.

10.00 p.m.—Arrive in Bastion. Good to see you again, old friend. Convoy to FOB Price in Gereshk tomorrow morning.

FRIDAY 29 OCTOBER

5.00 a.m.—Like that morning two years ago, we assemble before the flagpole at the centre of the Danish camp. Everybody is loaded up into vehicles. I am placed in a contraption that I have never seen before. It is a truck that has a large, armoured container on the back, the inside of which resembles a minibus with black seats and seatbelts. I climb in, buckle up, and resume listening to Tolkien's *The Silmarillion* on my iPod.

10.00 a.m.—Arrive at Price, desperately needing the toilet.

SUNDAY 31 OCTOBER

A small operation is happening tomorrow in the Green Zone. Gereshk is a fairly peaceful area, but I wonder if my theory about small operations will be proved right.

MONDAY 1 NOVEMBER

3.00 a.m.—Wake up and assemble in the large, dusty vehicle park by the entrance to FOB Price. It's a twenty-minute drive through the desert to reach the staging post. We dismount and begin to walk through the moonlight night toward the Green Zone. A nearby dog howls angrily at us. One of the Danes, heavily laden, falls into a stream as we each attempt to leap over it.

The first glimpses of another breathtaking Afghan dawn appear on the horizon. A nearby mosque comes to life, calling the local people to prayer. Intermittent Taliban radio chatter begins. Three Danish tanks suddenly appear at the top of a nearby ridge. Tanks are a rare thing in this country, and seldom see active duty. At the sight of these colossi, insurgent activity ceases immediately. Nobody, it seems, wants to mess with tanks.

5.00 p.m.—Finally make it back to base after a long, hot day. A fairly generic affair, but the Danes did find some bomb-making material, so it wasn't a total waste.

WEDNESDAY 3 NOVEMBER

Travel into Gereshk with a small Danish convoy to look at the work of an Afghan woman who employs other local women to help with various trades. In a culture dominated by males, this is a brave thing to do. Her groundskeeper, one of the few males in the building, tells me how the Taliban tried to attack several weeks ago, climbing over the wall. He chased them off with a shotgun. As I watch the woman talking to the Danes, I feel a twinge of sadness. Good people like this, who stick their head above the parapet to challenge convention in this country, rarely seem to last long. I wonder if she will still be alive twelve months from now.

FRIDAY 5 NOVEMBER

An early morning patrol round the various police checkpoints of Gereshk. At one of them, I am astonished to find an Afghan police officer lining his men up, and forcing them to urinate into small pots. He is testing them for drugs. The ANP has a reputation for being riddled with drug problems, and I have seen plenty of policemen on patrol over the last few years who are clearly under the influence of some narcotic or other. Seeing the ANP's own officers making a stand against drugs is a very encouraging sight.

4.00 p.m.—A Danish journalist named Bo arrives. He works for the Danish Defence Media Centre—the organization that started up NATO TV—and this is his first time here. He is a lovely chap, but I suspect that this is his first time in a conflict zone.

TUESDAY 9 NOVEMBER

Stories are scarce here. In desperation, I film a piece about the soldiers who guard Camp Price. They are Bosnians, and have only recently arrived in

Helmand. Despite the fact that guarding a gate is rather mundane, the fact that Bosnia, with all its war-torn past, is able to field soldiers—albeit only fifty of them—on a NATO operation is a significant thing. NATO HQ will love this, no doubt.

THURSDAY 11 NOVEMBER

Remembrance Day. The British and Danish soldiers congregate to have a brief memorial service. Gatherings like this are usually solemn affairs, and despite the fact that the soldiers are deployed in Afghanistan, they are told to be as smart as possible. Poor Bo, keen to get shots of the service but oblivious to the dress code, wanders around in shorts—a big military no-no for serious occasions. A Danish sergeant major spots him, and gives him some serious grief.

SUNDAY 14 NOVEMBER

Linking up with the Paras today. There will be a small British convoy going from FOB Price to Nahr-e-Serraj, the district where the Para Battalion is currently stationed. I have been given permission to ride in this convoy. It's another squashed affair in the back of a heavily armoured Mastiff, but I am glad for the protection. An IED strike now—so close to the end—would be absolutely devastating.

4.00 p.m.—Arrive at PB 2. It seems that whoever named the various patrol bases in Nahr-e-Serraj settled for fairly unimaginative monikers. Greeted by the sight of lots of fit young men in maroon T-shirts. I'm beginning to feel a little old. It's good to be back with the Paras.

MONDAY 15 NOVEMBER

Drive over to PB 1 to spend a few days there. I sit in the communal area, waiting for Matt, the officer in command of the Para company here, to finish a brief so I can introduce myself to him. Various other Paras gather, and I begin to worry about getting the surly looks and thinly veiled contempt that I received on my first trip with them in 2008. We get talking, and the customary 'how long have you been in Afghanistan?' question, which I make sure gets mentioned sooner rather than later, these days, actually manages to solicit some respect when I answer. Combine this with the fact that I am not as chubby as I was in 2008, and I seem to have got away quite lightly this time. Result.

TUESDAY 16 NOVEMBER

Out on patrol with the Paras in the local area. There have been several IED strikes out on the paths and fields surrounding PB 1, and I am careful where I tread. We stop while some Afghan soldiers—present on most patrols—stop and speak to a local farmer. One of the Paras turns to his friend. 'Hey, Jonesy. Even the cameraman looks more ally [cool] than you.' I pretend that I didn't hear the comment, but inside I am cheering. While this is a satisfying conclusion to one personal journey, it astounds me to think how much the issue of looking cool to professional soldiers has receded in my priorities since I first landed in this country. Quite simply, I have bigger things to care about these days.

WEDNESDAY 17 NOVEMBER

There is supposed to be a large joint patrol between the Afghan and British soldiers this afternoon. Rob, the British soldier who is in charge of mentoring the Afghans here, is glowing with praise about his charges. 'They are a really good bunch,' he enthuses. 'Hopefully you will see that this afternoon.'

2.00 p.m.—We meet by the entrance to PB 1. The Afghans arrive late—a customary practice for them. Their sergeant, a bad-tempered-looking man, becomes very angry when he is told that his men must lead the patrol. He argues—through an interpreter—that the British should go first. Rob patiently explains to him that the Afghans are also equipped with metal detectors, and that they must learn to lead, because the British aren't going to be around forever. The sergeant continues to argue, but Rob overrules him. He stalks away, sulking. We step out.

We cross small streams, dusty pathways, and cut through overgrown compounds. One compound is brimming with uncultivated marijuana plants. The British soldiers trade the customary jokes about how much they would like to pick them. The Afghans take it one step further, and actually do so. I can sense Rob becoming more and more irate.

We walk out into the open. BANG! BANG! Everybody whirls round, and I find myself instantly crouched, expecting Taliban fire to rake us at any second. There is a moment of silence. The Afghan sergeant stands with a lowered weapon, the barrel of which is still smoking. 'What were you shooting at?' Rob asks. The Paras are intently scanning the nearby land with their rifle scopes, looking for an enemy threat. The sergeant speaks to the interpreter, looking defiantly at Rob.

'Sir,' the interpreter says. 'He says that he was shooting at two children.'

'Children?!' Rob is almost screaming.

'Yes, sir. Children. He says that they were peeking at him from behind a rock, and because they were acting so suspiciously, he decided to shoot at them.' Rob has now turned red. 'Did it not occur to him that maybe the presence of thirty armed men made the children nervous, so they decided to hide?'

'No sir, it didn't.'

Rob swears loudly at the sergeant, and threatens him. It's a good job that the sergeant was so bad at shooting—both children are shaken but unharmed.

We slowly trudge back to base. Rob walks beside me. 'Forget what I said earlier, mate,' he pants as he walks—partly through exertion, partly through sheer fury—'They are a bunch of…'

The rest isn't worth repeating.

9.00 p.m.—Walking from my tent to the showers. I am only wearing flip-flops and a towel. CRACK! CRACK! CRACK! Incoming bullets from the Taliban whizz over the walls of the base. Red tracer rounds light up the night sky. I am not sure what to do. I think it's fairly unlikely that they could hit me, and it's not as if I can really run for cover with flip-flops on.

CRACKCRACKCRACK! BANG! BANG! The Paras return fire. It's too dark for me to film—Will has the night vision kit at the moment—and so I just decide to continue walking to the shower, despite the gunfight. Because of the commotion, the communal showers are empty, and I am able to enjoy a rinse in peace. If someone had told me two years ago that I'd be calmly strolling to take a shower in the middle of an exchange of bullets by this time in 2010 … how would I have felt?

THURSDAY 18 NOVEMBER

Patrol to a nearby checkpoint, where a platoon of Paras is holding a humanitarian gift day for the local children. In the distance, we see a long, colourful line of kids—including girls—making their way to the checkpoint. It's a poignant sight, seeing these fearsome Paras—many of whom have lost close friends over here—smiling as they hand over Wellington boots, gloves, scarves, hats, and various other pieces of winter clothing to the children, who will need them in the cold months to come. The innocence, the sheer joy of childhood reflected on those young faces, resonates with me as I watch them trundle back home with their arms full of gifts. This war is ugly, its future uncertain, but every now and then, at times like this, it brings out something worth celebrating. My miniscule part in this conflict is approaching its end. I wonder how it will all turn out in the years to come. Not my place to judge.

3.00 p.m.—Speak to Danielle on my mobile phone. I have to stand on Hesco blocks in a specific part of the base in order to get the minimum signal required to make a call.

She tells me that her ex has been in contact with her. He told her today that he doesn't want to be part of Jacob's life anymore, and that he isn't going to be able to visit her or Jacob from here on in. A wave of relief washes over me. I have spent countless nights worrying, wondering how we would work it out when we were married. I was determined—despite my misgivings—to try and love him in the way Jesus would want me to, and not to be the person who cuts him out of Jacob's life. It seems that he has chosen that for himself. I'm sure that this won't be the last we hear from him, but for now, it's a major weight off my mind. Thank you, Lord.

SATURDAY 20 NOVEMBER

Watch a British helicopter descend slowly into PB 2. Heading back to Bastion. That's it then, the last mission over. I'm not sure if I will ever ride in a helicopter again. I don't really mind either way. It has been a relatively quiet send-off, a fact that I am not bemoaning; the beginnings of a smooth segue into civilian life. Hopefully.

SUNDAY 21 NOVEMBER

Arrive back in Kabul. Begin to work on editing my Helmand stories.

WEDNESDAY 8 DECEMBER

Seeing that I was home last Christmas, it is my turn to stay here this time round. Will is going to be staying too—my makeshift brother for the last three years. Despite the cheer of each other's company, we're starting to really, profoundly struggle here. We feel that we have passed our Afghan expiry date and, although we're both too professional to say it outright, our hearts are just not in this place anymore. Being here is a daily grind to overcome the tide of overwhelming cynicism and despair tugging at our sense of reason. Cynicism at the way things here are conducted; despair that they stay the same despite endless suggestions that change is just around the corner. I suspect that Will won't be doing this for too much longer either. We've come a long way since we first met at Heathrow airport on a chilly morning in March 2008.

I am also fighting a running battle against letting my arrival home and the subsequent wedding day becoming my 'be-all and end-all', much like combat was a few years ago. When I let this replace God as my number one concern and source of joy, my morale invariably begins to plummet. It's a stern test.

MONDAY 13 DECEMBER

A guy called Bram is visiting us from NATO HQ. He is a self-confessed geek, and is here to fix our various ailing pieces of equipment. He also loves cats.

George saunters in, so dusty that his black coat looks light grey. Bram suggests that we bath him. Probably his first bath in years. Knowing the strength of George's claws, I wear my body armour and gloves as I try to shower him. He bellows at me in the feline equivalent of a horrible swear word. At least he is clean now.

SUNDAY 19 DECEMBER

The dear old chaplain, knowing that the end of my time here is drawing near, allows me to preach as much as I can. Tonight, the week before Christmas, I preach a sermon entitled 'The Four Loves of the First Christmas', which looks at the selfish love of King Herod, who wanted baby Jesus dead to further his own ends, the love displayed by the three wise men upon realising God's plan, the selfless love of Joseph, who decided not to get rid of Mary even though she had fallen pregnant, and finally the love of God that was demonstrated by Mary, who risked her life and reputation in order to obey God's will. As I preach, I think about the year to come. It's going to be a big change, going back to normal life. It will certainly be more comfortable. Will I love Danielle like Joseph loved Mary? Will I be passionate about seeking out God's plan in my life, like the wise men were? Will I love God above all else, and at whatever cost, like Mary? Or will I be a Herod? I pray it's the former.

The Taliban launch an attack in Kabul today—we can hear the explosions from the office. Five Afghan army officers die in the attack. Despite the relative safety of HQ, I find that I am becoming more and more nervous that something is going to happen to me, right at the end of the race. I have no interest in testing my courage anymore. That part of my story finished a long while back.

FRIDAY 24 DECEMBER

Christmas Eve service at the chapel. It feels rather odd, even untraditional to be playing a guitar at a candlelit service like this, but needs must. Will even attends too, despite the fact that he isn't really into church. It's a special evening.

Receive an e-card from Fahran, wishing me 'Merry Christmas'. It's a huge relief to hear from him after so long. He tells me that he is staying with a family in France at the moment, and that things seem to be going well for him. It looks like he may not be coming back here, after all.

SATURDAY 25 DECEMBER

Will and I spend the day together, merrily churning through one of our bad film marathons, and generally trying not to feel sorry for ourselves. The lunch that is served by the caterers is truly awful, and we return to our rooms without eating much. Still, it must be better than the lot of those poor soldiers stuck out in the middle of nowhere, with only rations to eat today. We try to persuade a cat, one of George's friends, to join us for the day. In a flurry of meowing protest, he rudely declines. Cats have no manners.

Not long to go now.

FRIDAY 31 DECEMBER

New Year's Eve. Spend the evening with Danielle on Skype. We think back to New Year's Eve twelve months ago, where we had our first cuddle and watched the fireworks in London. We try to forget the long, crowded slog home. In a way, this last year has gone very fast. In another, it has been painfully slow. Either way, I am glad that it is almost up.

MONDAY 3 JANUARY

I'll be flying home next week. The sky has been completely clear every day for several weeks now. Despite this, I am worried about a winter snowstorm, which is far from rare in Kabul during these months, suddenly descending and grounding all the flights.

TUESDAY 11 JANUARY

Every morning, I run outside and check the sky. It is beginning to get cloudy. Check the forecast. Snow is predicted later this week. No. No. No. No. Is the weather going to conspire to do what nothing else could, to stop me from getting home? If I think logically, a delay wouldn't really be that bad, but I am so weary of this place that logic doesn't count for much anymore. I just want out now. I am done with Afghanistan.

Despite my worries, I know that if I have learnt nothing else during my time here, I have learnt to trust God, and to give the future over to him.

WEDNESDAY 12 JANUARY

Flight booked for tomorrow. I spend the day packing my bags and cleaning out my room. I'm not the tidiest person in the world (by which I mean that any space I inhabit degrades into a hideous swamp of discarded socks within days), so it's a lengthy process. The amount of odds and ends that I have acquired during my nigh-on three years here astounds me. Pouches, belts, knives, torches, backpacks, wires. The list goes on. Each item has a story attached to it, most involving a random, desperate experience in some distant FOB, and subsequent reluctance to get rid of the object in question out of sentimentality. Choosing what gets into my final luggage contingent for the flight home—a relatively small load—is a mildly heartbreaking experience. Despite my weariness with this country, it's going to be a big shock coming home to real life.

THURSDAY 13 JANUARY

4.00 p.m.—This is it. The end of an era. Mel and Ruth, who have returned from their Christmas leave and sent Will off on his, accompany me to the airport in a taxi—a ceremonial guard of sorts. I exit the taxi, and give them both a hug. Usually, any sort of public contact between a man and a woman is frowned upon here. Even now, I can feel the gaze of several ANP on us. I don't care, they are my family. We have been through so much together. We say our goodbyes, and I head toward the check-in.

I have packed my pockets full of pens—prepared to bribe my way onto the plane if the guards bemoan the fact that I am ISAF. Oh well; I just want to get on the flight, no matter how much stationery it costs me. I reach passport control. The guard duly stamps my passport, and sends me on my way. That was actually remarkably easy. Didn't even ask for a staple.

Board the plane. Taxi down runway. I look out of the window, half expecting to see the blue uniforms of police charging toward the plane in a final, comedic bid to stop me, or the Taliban letting loose one last, poorly aimed RPG to get me. Nope, just tarmac. Take off. Breathe a huge sigh of relief.

Watch the beautiful Afghan mountains shrink beneath me in the fading light. I think back to when I first set eyes on them, out the window of the Danish flight to Kabul on 2 April 2 2008. So much has happened to me since then. I don't recognize the Josh I was back then, and I doubt he would recognize me. I think of the experiences I have had—the close calls, the terror during firefights, the closeness of friends, the warmth of love. It has been one heck of a ride.

Most of all, above and beyond the adventures that I have had, it's the fact that God has used this time to turn my heart back to him that hits me the hardest. He has brought me through pain, combat, fear, and loss. He has transformed my life. Out of nowhere, he has given me the best girl in the world, and a gorgeous baby boy to boot. I cannot wait to spend the rest of my life with them. God has taught me that he alone can be trusted, utterly. He has taught me that putting him first is the way to true happiness—not chasing combat, drink, women, or excitement. I didn't deserve his love, kindness, or favour, and yet he poured it out on me because he loves me.

That's it. That's what grace is.

Epilogue: Endings and Beginnings

SATURDAY 2 APRIL 2011

The big day is finally here. I stand at the top of the church, waiting for Danielle to walk through the doors. Tradition dictates that the groom faces away from the bride as she walks up the aisle. Forget that, I have waited far too long and have been through far too much to not treasure this moment in my memories hereafter. Looking around the gathered people in the church, I see so many people who mean so much to me. Will, my dear friend and brother throughout the Afghan experience, stands holding a camera—he kindly agreed to film the ceremony for me. Ruth, David, and his fiancé Laura sit, smiling at me. Mel sent me her apologies several days ago; she is stuck in Helmand, and is not able to make it back in time, but she is here in spirit. I see my family—my dear mum and dad, grandmother and uncle, who prayed for me every day while I was in Afghanistan, my brothers and sister, firm friends and confidants. My old school friends and church members who supported Danielle and me through love, friendship, and prayer in this past year.

The music starts. The doors open, and the most beautiful sight I have ever seen walks in. Danielle looks absolutely radiant; I cannot believe that she actually wants to marry this mad, balding fellow. I have waited so long for this that my mind almost overloads as I try to process what I am seeing.

In a film, this would be the golden ending, the moment when the picture fades out and the credits begin to roll, leaving the leading man and leading lady to live happily ever after. Although I have been looking forward to this for over a year, I know that this is only just the beginning. Like my pursuit of combat two years ago, where I thought that I would be finally happy if I got in a firefight, I warn myself not to fall into the same trap. I cannot wait to be married. I cannot wait for all the good things that come with marriage. But, I cannot afford to take my eyes off God. As I move into this new stage of life, with all its new challenges and trials, I must remember to love him more than anything else—even my new family—and to trust in him above all other things—even Danielle. He has promised never to leave me or forsake me.

My dad—who is conducting the service—pronounces us man and wife. 'You may kiss the bride,' he says, grinning at us. We throw ourselves into each other's arms and lock lips. Everybody claps and cheers.

One adventure has ended. Another has just begun.

'You may kiss the bride!'

'Ally'	Army slang for 'cool'
ANA	Afghan National Army
ANCOP	Afghan National Civil Order Police
ANP	Afghan National Police
CNN	Central News Network
CNS	Camp Nathan Smith
BAF	Bagram Airfield
BBC	British Broadcasting Corporation
BSN	Camp Bastion
COIN	Counter Insurgency
DANCON	Danish Contingent
FLET	Forward Line of Enemy Troops
FSG	Fire Support Group
FMC	Forsvarets Mediecenter, the Danish Defence Media Agency
FOB	Forward Operating Base
HLS	Helicopter Landing Site
IED	Improvised Explosive Device
ISAF	International Security Assistance Force, the face of NATO in Afghanistan
JTAC	Joint Terminal Air Controller
LN	Local National
LZ	Landing Zone
KAF	Kandahar Airfield
KAIA	Kabul International Airport
KIA	Killed In Action
MOD	Ministry Of Defence
MPAT	Mobile Public Affairs Team
NATO	North Atlantic Treaty Organization
NDS	National Directorate of Security
NSE	National Support Element, the part of a base belonging to a specific nation
OMLT	Operational Mentoring and Liaison Team
PAX	Another, easier word for 'person'
PB	Patrol Base
RPG	Rocket Propelled Grenade

RSM	Regimental Sergeant Major
SAS	Special Air Service
SF	Special Forces
TIC	Troops In Contact, i.e. in a firefight with the enemy
'Turd'	A nickname for a fairly uninteresting story
WIA	Wounded In Action